COLORADO MARIJUANA REAL ESTATE

COLORADO MARIJUANA REAL ESTATE

Work from Home

Jay Hidoshi

ISBN-13: 9781508850472
ISBN-10: 150885047X

Acknowledgments

Cover Design: Rita Toews
Cover Image: Jay Hidoshi
Book Formatting: Createspace
Book Editor: Susan Mary Malone
Interior Images: Jay Hidoshi

View the photo gallery and the full Web site for this book:
coloradomjrealestate.com

On the cover:
The author grew this medical-marijuana extended plant count of ninety-nine on much less than one quarter of an acre. Three years after being purchased, this Colorado medical marijuana home sold for sixty percent more than market value. The main nutrients for this crop: *FoxFarm* basic nutrient line of *GrowBig, TigerBloom, and BigBloom* at half strength or less. This neighborhood grows medical marijuana.

About The Author

J ay Hidoshi was the owner of a medical marijuana dispensary in Denver, Colorado for seven years. The dispensary sold seven years from purchase at almost 300% more.

Jay Hidoshi has been a resident of Colorado for twenty-four years and has three Colorado businesses.

This book gives insight about Colorado marijuana real estate. Equally important, it's for all who are interested in how legal marijuana evolved from 2001 to 2014.

This book is instructional and informative on the subject of the marijuana industry in Colorado. It gives some growing secrets of the medical marijuana dispensary.

View the photo gallery and much more information at the Web site for this book: coloradomjrealestate.com

Jay Hidoshi can be consulted at: coloradommjrealestate@gmail.com

Table Of Contents

Introduction

This book touches on medical marijuana dispensaries only to show how they paved the way for Colorado Amendment 64, otherwise known as 'Recreational Pot'.

The discussion of medical marijuana dispensaries in this book is partly to show that as a business format for the recreational marijuana retail business. The medical marijuana caregiver started in and still exists in the home.

A caregiver is a person taking care of the health of a patient. Under Colorado regulations, this can mean as little as helping with a patient's meal or transportation. A caregiver can also provide and grow medical marijuana for the patients. The medical marijuana dispensary is owned by a caregiver or partnership of caregivers.

This book refers to the medical marijuana dispensary to show the ways to cut costs in the growing of marijuana, and still be just as productive.

This book also explains that 'activists' are the ones who made history. The book explains how marijuana farmers (activists) forced the Colorado State government to set up regulations in order to keep the Feds out and keep Colorado a good example in the media.

What came first, the chicken or the egg? This book explains that the medical marijuana dispensary came first. The Colorado State Regulations were adopted from medical marijuana dispensaries that are role models in the State of Colorado.

The big picture should be: If people can Legalize Marijuana, are they capable of making other changes to the USA, if not the entire world? Is it possible to get politicians to represent the people? Yes, but you may have to give them a big job that overwhelms them like marijuana or same-sex marriage. Otherwise, all their time is consumed spending and patting themselves on the back.

This book is only partly for the use of growing marijuana from your home in the great State of Colorado. The great part of Colorado marijuana under amendment 20 and amendment 64 is that home growing is allowed in Colorado. In many other states and the world it is prohibited and people must go to a dispensary to get marijuana. [1]

This book gives information and insight on the topic of Colorado marijuana real estate. Although there is a specific chapter on this, it will also give insight on this topic throughout the entire book. Including residential and commercial real estate.

If you have no interests in growing marijuana but want to know how marijuana was able to become legal, then this book explains the chronological steps of Colorado medical marijuana caregiver to the Colorado Recreational Pot stores.

This book will explain the *do* and *don'ts* of medical-marijuana and recreational pot.

It explains 'early flowering products' and *incredible marijuana bud density.* Making it all worthwhile, when going to the scale.

The author's favorite marijuana-growing recipe and growing products.

1

The Legalization Of Marijuana In The Great State Of Colorado-Amendment 64

On November 6, 2012, the voters of the Great State of Colorado voted for Amendment 64. Votes totaled 2,500,033, of that 1,383,139 were *yes* votes to the 1,116, 894 *no* votes. That is fifty-five point thirty-two percent *yes* votes. On December 10, 2012, Governor 'Hickenlooper' signed the Declaration of Amendment 64 as part of the Colorado State Constitution. Dispensaries served legal marijuana to the world on January 1, 2014.

The truth is, the politicians did not legalize marijuana in Colorado. Marijuana and the medical marijuana farmers did. When you have more medical marijuana farmers practicing their rights to grow medical marijuana, it creates more supply for more users (demand).

As of January 1, 2014, the legalization of marijuana in the Great State of Colorado exists, and has taken monster baby steps for the world. Recreational Pot, Amendment 64 has a long ways to go. A lot of case law will occur defining Amendment 64 as time passes. Medical marijuana and Amendment 64 can be compared to same-sex marriages when it comes to how the states of the United States will all handle medical marijuana in the future.[2] My opinion is that same-sex marriage will be a burden to a state's economy, where marijuana or medical marijuana stimulates it. "Could marijuana turn the USA economy around by forty percent?" I think there might be a couple of people thinking that.

Medical marijuana will continue to become legal in more states in the USA, because of case law. The way that it ultimately became legal under medical marijuana was through the approval of a medical doctor for a patient to use marijuana as a medicine of choice–just as all American citizens have a choice of all types of other medicines.

Ultimately, governments at all levels–federal, state, county, and city–do not make money unless some kind of state economy exists. Government relies on the revenue of marijuana and medical marijuana. Just another reason marijuana is legal in the State of Colorado. Government claims that law enforcement spends all its time locking people up when marijuana is illegal. The fact is, now that marijuana is legal, law enforcement will bring in more in revenue on driving offenses with DWAI's (Driving While Ability Impaired) alone.[3]

Recreational pot in Colorado will be referred to in this book as 'Amendment 64' and vise versa.

Amendment 64 allows the use of marijuana by adults twenty-one years or older. It is legal to grow six marijuana plants with only three in flower. The marijuana plants must be grown in a secure lockable area. It is legal to transport one ounce. It is also legal to give one ounce as a gift to other citizens twenty-one years or older.

Visitors and tourists of Colorado can use and purchase marijuana but can not take it out of the state.

Amendment 64 allows an individual twenty-one or older to grow the six marijuana plants of other twenty-one year olds. The city of Denver has an ordinance that allows a maximum of twelve total plants per residence, regardless of the number of adults living in the home.[3B] It is almost guaranteed that all cities and townships will set some limit to the amount of marijuana plants allowed per home.

The very reason that caregivers of Colorado can grow the medical marijuana plants for patients is the same reason a person should be able to grow the six plants for others under Amendment 64. The reasons under medical marijuana are because the patient does not have the space to grow six medical marijuana plants. The patient does not have the money to grow six medical marijuana plants; the patient does not have legs and is 'restricted'. The reasons really can be for any reason, technically. The same reasons (any reason) should be entitled to farmers of legal marijuana to grow others' six plants. Higher plant counts are an option with the practice of medical marijuana.

Under Medical Marijuana in Colorado (Amendment 20), the designated caregiver should possess copies of the paperwork of the patients he/she is growing medical marijuana for.[4] The proper paperwork is submitted to the Colorado Department of Public Health and Environment, Medical Marijuana Registry for approval annually.[5] This process will be taught in chapter four.

Under Amendment 64, technically things are still far from legal. If you look at a business model under other so-called legal businesses, you will see that the manufacturing of any given product is not limited (for example, beer is not limited in the volume that it is manufactured, steel is not limited to the volume that it is manufactured, bricks, etc.). The state of Colorado has determined how many recreational pot plants a twenty-one year old can grow but most cities and towns will copy Denver's ordinance of twelve plants per household.

The bottom line is that under *legal* business practice with other legal business models, no limitations on manufacturing exists and the price is determined by supply and demand.

It is understandable why marijuana is over regulated. The laws and regulations are all new to the entire world. The fact is that when the medical marijuana *boom* was taking place in Colorado around the years of 2005 to 2008, some attorneys were part owners of medical marijuana dispensaries. It was the win-win situation for the medical marijuana dispensary. The dispensary saved a lot of money on attorney fees for legal advice, and the attorney would make a lot of money being part owner/ investor. The attorney also advised that the business should do things a certain way pertaining to business practice, because that is what the State of Colorado would accept as reasonable business practice from these types of businesses in the future.

The medical marijuana dispensaries that are role models in the industry are the ones that actually created the Colorado State Regulations for Medical Marijuana. The politicians just adopted what they liked from the dispensaries they liked. The politicians are still patting themselves on the back for such a fine job they have done with all this. Just like they pat themselves on the back for everything else they have done (ex: Spending out of control).

Colorado Governor Hickenlooper signed a Declaration of Amendment 64 as part of Colorado State Constitution. Governor Hickenlooper knows how to make money. Not all politicians know how to make money, but it is safe to say Governor Hickenlooper does. He also knows that Colorado has a history of a depressed economy in the 1980s. The media has reported that Governor Hickenlooper has made hypocritical statements. The media has also slandered him as a 'Saloon Keeper'.[7] The facts are, now that he is governor, he really was just doing his job. The voters are the ones who made marijuana legal. Governor Hickenlooper is just a politician who knows how to make money. The phrase Decision Maker suites him better. All politicians are decision makers. Some politicians are horrible. But across the world after they all make their decisions, the world still turns. *Amen*

Amendment 64 has a ways to go. A person can very well get the feel for how to grow marijuana under Amendment 64. For those who want to grow more than six plants, the option of medical marijuana allows for higher plant counts. Marijuana in this book will sometimes be abbreviated to 'mj'. Medical Marijuana will sometimes be abbreviated as 'MMJ' or 'medical mj'.

Amendment 20 Colorado Medical Marijuana

Colorado Amendment 64, Recreational Marijuana, was able to have Colorado state regulations and laws in place in a prompt amount of time. The State of Colorado only allowed medical marijuana dispensaries to sell the Recreational Pot on January 1, 2014. This means the business is already operating as a medical marijuana dispensary under Amendment 20, and has the option to operate under Amendment 64 with the purchase of the recreational retail licenses. Both medical patients and recreational users potentially go in to the dispensary. This medical marijuana dispensary format has been seeing new regulations year after year. To allow a very similar business to operate out of an existing business format makes for a quick infrastructure that is already in place. Not only is it in place, the federal government is leaving it alone. It is my opinion that they would start a war if they tried to stop it. The only thing they can do now is get revenue off marijuana. Marijuana people are peaceful and nonviolent but you could say that marijuana in Colorado has steamrolled through and nothing will stop it now.

Amendment 20 amended the Colorado State Constitution to allow the use of marijuana for patients with medical consent from a doctor.[4] Under Amendment 20, a patient may possess up to two ounces of medical marijuana and may grow six medical marijuana plants (with only three in flower). The use of medical marijuana is allowed by people of the age of eighteen or older. Medical marijuana patients are approved by the medical marijuana registry and patients and caregivers receive a Colorado Medical Marijuana Card (RED CARD).

Doctors can make the right to the State of Colorado of the patient's specific medical needs to possess and grow more medical marijuana. Patients caught with more than two ounces in their possession can argue 'medical necessity'.

These are all conditions recognized for the use of medical marijuana in Colorado: Cachexia, cancer, chronic pain, chronic nervous system disorders, epilepsy, seizures, glaucoma, HIV or AIDS, multiple sclerosis, and disorders from muscle spasms and nausea. Medical marijuana patients may not use medical marijuana in public or plain view or operate a vehicle or machinery after the use of medical marijuana. Medical marijuana patients may obtain medical marijuana from a caregiver or a medical marijuana dispensary. Consuming marijuana or medical marijuana in public, under Denver Public Municipal Ordinance and under Colorado State Law, brings in a fine of $100.00, if ticketed.[8]

Most states will most likely practice medical marijuana in the future. The choice to use a certain medicine over another is an individual's right as long as the doctor has approved the medicine for the condition. It is silly for a patient to have the choice of Valium, codeine, oxycodone, etc., etc., etc., and not have the right to use medical marijuana.

This will all lay out state by state as case law is presented in the courtroom.

3

Knowing the truth about the legality of growing, buying, selling, transporting, and consumption of Recreational Pot and Medical Marijuana in Colorado.

With all the teaching techniques of this book, you will be able to get maximum yield from six marijuana plants. If you want to grow more than six plants, then medical marijuana is an option. This book teaches medical marijuana also.

Growing, buying, selling, transporting, and consuming medical mj is still illegal under USA Federal Law. The following information allows you to protect yourself under Colorado state laws. If the governor of the great State of Colorado can sign a Declaration of Amendment 64 as part of the Colorado Constitution, then you can actively follow the regulations. Colorado's medical marijuana regulations are creating a new wheel for the rest of the nation's states to follow. It also paved the way for Amendment 64 in Colorado. The feds generally leave law-abiding citizens alone, specifically for the growing of medical marijuana and recreational pot. Recreational pot has only been in place since January 1, 2014. The sale of two ounces of marijuana or less has been decriminalized in the State of Colorado. Five to one hundred pounds of marijuana is illegal under Federal law, with an even stiffer sentence for the sale of 100 pounds or more.

It is highly unlikely that someone would get a summons for growing marijuana, as long as you are following Colorado state laws.

The federal government is leaving medical marijuana and Amendment 64 alone because of the regulations in place. Although different, this is similar to how the federal government is leaving states alone for same-sex marriages.

One purpose of this book is to teach anyone interested how to grow large crops of medical marijuana, from home as a Colorado caregiver. It really does not give instruction for opening a medical marijuana dispensary because in Colorado those state licenses are currently not being sold by the state. Also, currently it is required in some Colorado cities and towns to have a State of Colorado Medical Marijuana Dispensary License as a prerequisite/ requirement to purchase a recreational pot license. If this route is taken, you will have to have large capital assets in order to open a medical mj dispensary.[6] Colorado medical mj dispensaries have held their value for resale due to the state's decision only to allow medical mj dispensaries to have the option of buying the 2014 recreational marijuana retail state licenses.

The medical marijuana dispensaries that have not purchased the recreational pot licenses may be interested in selling to investors who do want to buy the recreational pot license. As of July 1, 2014, only certain cities and towns will require the prerequisite of the medical marijuana dispensary licenses.

The author was the owner of a medical marijuana dispensary and is part of a network of other dispensary owners. Occasionally there are Colorado medical marijuana dispensaries for sale, and the author can be consulted for this information.

The State of Colorado will eventually have the legal pot/recreational pot shop state license for sale to business people outside of the current owners of medical marijuana dispensaries. These recreational pot-shop state licenses will be limited in numbers, based on the towns and cities of Colorado and the ordinances they put in place for restrictions as to how far apart these businesses have to be from each other (example 1000 feet apart). The best way to be eligible with the State of Colorado to purchase the Colorado recreational pot license outside of the medical marijuana dispensary state license is to acquire a retail-business property lease, or own a retail-business space before you apply for the state licenses for retail recreational pot. This lease or owner's deed would of course have to be 1000 feet away from a school (this also applies to Colorado caregivers growing at home.) Churches can be schools if they have children's classes, so do your research. The State of Colorado will sell recreational pot state licenses to those who have the oldest leases or deeds that fit the proper guidelines for marijuana retail property setbacks to schools, etc.

Only allowing medical marijuana dispensaries to purchase the Colorado recreational pot state license for Jan. 1, 2014, allows the State of Colorado to build some revenue to regulate and enforce recreational pot. It also allows Colorado counties, cities, and townships to build their individual ordinances for recreational pot. By allowing medical marijuana dispensaries to purchase the state license for recreational pot allows the State of Colorado to regulate more easily due to tighter regulations on medical marijuana dispensaries since about 2007, depending on the many dispensaries that exist.

Although, under Colorado state law, medical marijuana dispensaries and recreational pot have been legalized through regulations, individual cities and townships can still decide to ban these marijuana businesses.[10] Under Colorado state law, cities and townships have the option to ban medical marijuana dispensaries and recreational pot shops within city and town limits, but they cannot ban the growing of medical marijuana of an individual 'caregiver' from homes. Colorado cities and townships can set ordinances on medical marijuana plant limits grown by a caregiver. [11]

The State of Colorado is literally in the process of inventing the wheel. One example is the state-run banking system they have proposed for medical mj dispensaries/recreational pot shops. Although dispensaries have already been leaving a paper trail to show accounting and tax returns, traditionally this has been a cash business. By implementing a state-run banking system for the dispensaries/ recreational pot shops, it says to the federal government that the Coloradans are following state laws and the State of Colorado is trying to keep track of the money. The State of Colorado has set up many ways for their regulations on medical mj and recreational pot in order to keep the federal government out. Consultation can be pursued with the author on dispensaries or any other topics in this book. Email contact for the author: coloradommjrealestate@gmail.com

As of July 1, 2014, there will be no prerequisite of having the medical marijuana dispensary license for the purchase of the recreational pot license. Some individual cities and towns may make it policy that MMJ dispensary license prerequisite still exist.

This book gives information on what to look for in a property if leasing or buying for the purpose of growing marijuana. This book gives insight on the Colorado marijuana network and also includes information for the individual who really just wants to go to work and make an honest living. This book has instructions for those who have an interest in growing six marijuana plants under Amendment 64 or medical marijuana at the caregiver level. Both can be done from home. It also will explain 'extended plant counts' under Amendment 20. For anyone who wants to grow six Legal marijuana plants under the guidelines of Colorado Amendment 64, the instructions for medical marijuana should be followed for maximum yield.[12]

One of the biggest reasons medical mj is legal under Colorado state law is because of activists/ caregivers who were willing to go to jail for their risks in this new venture we call medical mj. Twenty percent of Colorado's population is growing medical marijuana or recreational pot or both. You do the math. Even the feds would have a hard time locking up that many citizens. An activist is not a talking head, but rather one who does what he says. For example, a medical mj farmer. (This book is dedicated to all the citizens who are not cowards and grow marijuana.) The citizens of Colorado in 2001, when Amendment 20 was in place, know there was a lot less growing of medical marijuana then. All the growers combined show what it means to be an activist. Anyone in Colorado during the years 2000-2003 knows that caregivers were still getting locked up for growing medical marijuana. Some of those victims have received restitution through the courts.

Chances are that recreational marijuana regulations may change for the better in the future as regulations change year after year. My opinion of medical mj is more legal under federal guidelines than recreational pot. The reason being that medical mj is medicine and recreational pot is not medicine. Medical marijuana has been in place since 2001 and has been much more regulated since that date. You will also be able to make an annual income easier under medical mj as a caregiver than a Colorado recreational-pot farmer, at the current time. Next is the process of medical mj, the Red Card, and how to obtain the proper paperwork to grow large amounts of medical marijuana. This book and the author have no intentions of teaching the practice of breaking the law.

4

The Colorado Medical
Marijuana Card

If you just want to grow recreational marijuana under Colorado laws, then following the recipe for medical marijuana will work on your marijuana plants. If you have a reason to use medical marijuana, and want the option to grow more than six recreational pot plants, then medical marijuana is for you.

In most cases you have to be of eighteen years old or older to apply for a Colorado Medical Marijuana Card. You will find ninety-nine percent of the information needed to apply for the Colorado Medical Marijuana Card on the Colorado Department of Public Health and Environment website.[5] Once at the site, click 'Medical Marijuana Forms'. Most citizens will select 'Form # MMR 1001'. A total of three pages need to be filled out *exactly* the way that the CDPHE wants them filled out. For the first time you apply and all the other times that you renew, pay the extra money at the doctor's office to have them fill out all three pages. The CDPHE can change the forms sometimes as often as every year. The doctor's office knows how the CDPHE wants the forms sent in. If you get rejected from the CDPHE, it's usually because of a clerical mistake at the doctor's office. If for some reason this is not the case, then the doctor's office will figure out what the CDPHE wants in order for your application to be processed. It may sound complicated, but it's not. The law is that in Colorado, you have the right to choose medical marijuana just like you have the right to choose oxycodone, codeine, Valium, or any other drug.

Although it could take you a little while to conceivably have the paperwork to grow 600 medical marijuana plants, it is a reality to conceivably get the paperwork for 200 medical marijuana plants your first year. Some doctors will write extended plant counts for one hundred per patient for a price. They are not easy to find.

The Red Card, as it is known in Colorado, is valid for one year. In order to obtain a Medical Marijuana Red Card, one must first have a valid Colorado State ID card or Colorado driver license. If someone enters into the State of Colorado and wants to retain his drivers license from the state of origin, then his option is to present a residential lease agreement dated for the same year that the medical marijuana Red Card is being applied for, and the lease prepared on behalf of the property owner of Colorado. This lease would have to read in a manner that the tenant is not restricted to grow marijuana on the premises of the rental property in order to grow medical marijuana or recreational pot.

Examples that a temporary resident of Colorado may want to retain his driver's license from the State where he resides full time are: #1) An attorney practices law in Florida and needs to retain his Florida driver license in order to continue practicing law in Florida. #2) A general contractor is required to have a contractor's license in the state that she is from and needs to retain her driver's license from the state she resides, in full-time, in order to keep the contractor's license in place.

By the way, all walks of life use medical marijuana and the information you provide to the 'CDPHE' is strictly information of the Medical Marijuana Registry. This information is only allowed access by a court judge. Just like any other drug that you may take, this information is only between you and your doctor. The information you provide to friends or family or associates would be voluntary.

Legal recreational pot needs no documents at all, other than a government-issued ID showing that the individual is twenty-one years old in order to follow the laws of Amendment 20.

Under Colorado state law, the medical mj card is obtained by a visit to one of the many medical doctors in Colorado. An on-line search of 'MMJ doctors in Colorado' will bring up a few. The most common way that the medical marijuana card is obtained from a medical doctor is for the reasons of chronic pain. The Red Card allows for the use of medical mj for severe pain due to a debilitating medical condition. One of the reasons you may choose medical mj over other drugs such as oxycodone is that oxycodone can cause nausea and vomiting. Lots of bad pharmaceutical drugs are on the market and approved by the FDA. The FDA approved those because of pharmaceutical drug-company lobbyists. The population is starting to realize that medical marijuana is a more *natural* medicine. It is superior to any sleeping pill that exists. Although medical marijuana still to this day gets smeared in the media, it is mostly due to a need for something to fill news time slots.

Severe pain may result in other problems, such as insomnia. Back and neck conditions can not only be ongoing, but in a lot of cases, can be documented on doctor's records, for decades if not a lifetime. Shoulders, knees, elbows, osteoporosis, degenerative disk disease, arthritis, etc., etc., *all cause severe pain.* The general public in the USA that can afford health insurance has caught on to the huge profits that surgeons make and that surgery may not always be the best solution. Managing pain with whatever system works for you has become the trend. Cancer and HIV are givens for the medical use of medical mj.

Medical records such as MRIs and x-rays are no longer required by the state of Colorado at the time of doctor visits. But to bring these documents to the doctor on your first visit isn't a bad idea. It shows the doctor that you are an adult. Patients who have tattoos and body piercings, such as pierced noses and tongues, may be declined by the doctor for the extended plant count. This is a stereotypical world, and doctors have been known to decline requests to anyone based on the way he looks.

The older you are, chances are you will have more recent documents to show your ailments. Kids eighteen or older usually do not have these types of pain problems unless (for example) they are in a car or motorcycle accident. It helps to do the research of which doctors have been around a while and plan on staying around. Although not required, it is also a good idea to stay with the same doctor year after year, just as you would with other doctors because they do a good job for you.

The conditions recognized by the state of Colorado are one of the reasons that it is more legal to grow medical marijuana in Colorado than any other state. The amount of conditions and the use for chronic pain separates Colorado from many other medical marijuana states.

COLORADO CAREGIVERS

The Red Card can also qualify you as a caregiver and under Colorado state law allows five patients per caregiver. The one-to-five patients designate the caregiver with the MMJ registry. Although not required, the important thing is that caregivers keep their same patients year after year, making on paper long-lasting relationship. A caregiver should be able to grow plenty of mj with as little as two to three patients. As a Colorado caregiver under medical marijuana regulations, a caregiver can grow the amount of medical marijuana on his or her extended plant count and the extended plant counts of that caregiver's five patients. Even without an extended plant count, a Colorado caregiver can grow six medical marijuana plants and the six plants of his five patients. That is thirty-six medical marijuana plants with eighteen in flower at a time.

The amount of patients a caregiver can have has been a larger number in the past. For the year 2014, it is currently five patients to one caregiver. The state regulations can and do change but there is a proposed number of ten patients to one caregiver for the year 2015, currently undetermined.

In the great state of Colorado, you can grow more medical marijuana than in any other state in the USA. You also get to live in the most beautiful state in the USA.

With a medical mj red card, you will be able to grow six plants. But under an extended plant count, doctors have been known to write as high as one hundred plants per patient. Although these doctors are hard to find, the norm for an extended plant count is seventy to seventy-five plants per patient. Both of these counts will be of additional fees. Other known extended plant counts that may or may not have additional fees are the twelve, eighteen, thirty-two, forty-eight plant counts. Do your research. Some doctors may or may not charge extra fees for these lower-number extended plant counts. All doctors charge different amounts but are usually close to the same price.

The most common way that extended plant counts are obtained is through the reasons to the physician that medical mj is being used for edible use.

Edible use means the person does not choose to smoke medical mj but ingests by eating or drinking.

Once you move to Colorado, you will have plenty of inexpensive medical mj so that you will be able to eat as much as you want. Edibles can be eaten in the form of brownies or tincture. Once edibles are used on a daily basis, the body can build a tolerance to the Tetrahydrocannabinol (THC). The THC in edibles is generally of a much stronger content than the THC content of a mj cigarette known as a joint, blunt, doobie, spliff, etc. With a higher tolerance, the body may require higher doses of THC in order for the THC to be effective. This is an additional reinforcing reason why a doctor would write an extended plant count for additional plants for edible use.

In order to make very potent edibles, the use of the entire medical mj buds may also need to be used, depending on factors such as the farmer's experience in farming MMJ, crop problems, strain was not potent, etc.

Technically, edible use means that the entire plant and the entire crop is being used for edible or infused products in order to make high quality, potent edibles or infused products. Do not get paranoid, these records are not accessible to anyone. Only a judge can access these documents and a court order is necessary to do so. All your medical information is confidential, just as it is between you and your doctors.

Keep in mind under Colorado state law a caregiver is technically supposed to do something other than just grow medical mj for his patients. It is so vague in the Colorado statute that it could mean as little as helping patient's fix a meal, help in getting something from the store, help with transportation, etc. By now you have probably done the math, and are saying god that's a lot of plants. Originally, medical doctors in Colorado prescribed this many plants partially due to the fact that most people were not capable of growing that many healthy plants and they were not capable of growing the medical mj plants more than two to three feet high. That has changed. It's a money-making deal on both sides. The doctors are making money and the farmers are too. I don't think anyone can put a number on the amount on how much medical mj has stimulated the Colorado state economy. Many will agree that Colorado's economy is booming, including the governor.[9]

Keep your Colorado medical marijuana card up to date and manage all your patients' MMJ paperwork that you may have. If for some reason you let your medical marijuana card expire and you get in trouble, contact the author of this book for the top two attorneys recommended in this field. I will recommend them because they get the job done, one hundred percent of the time.

Many medical mj attorneys exist in Colorado, whom the author can refer based on the Colorado case law that has taken place thus far. *If* convicted of cultivation of one hundred plants or more under federal law, guidelines start at a five-year jail sentence. This is very rare in the state of Colorado because under medical marijuana and the extended plant count you are abiding by Colorado state law. Even if you are above plant count of ninety-nine, you would still be within state law under the extended plant count and the pretense of medicine. This number ninety-nine is a number that is commonly used amongst Colorado caregivers. Some go over ninety-nine and some do not. It's the ones going way, way over who would be at high risk.

I personally have had up to one hundred fifty outdoor plants. The county sheriff was flying over my property one morning in a helicopter. He circled around twice. He could have called the feds to bust me but he didn't. The truth is that there is a lot of greed in the marijuana business. Much larger farms exist and those are the ones they look for. Not just on private land but on public National Forest and BLM land. You could say the feds have their hands full with extremely large marijuana farms and this includes the Mexican cartel before MMJ was even legal in Colorado.

The ninety-nine medical mj plant count applies to Colorado caregivers who have reason to believe they could be being watched by the feds (are you paranoid?). It would also apply to individuals growing marijuana crops so large they would be in excess of one hundred pounds.

Almost all the paranoia is gone in Colorado. It's a job, now. This book will try to explain that to the world, so everyone can see the comfort level in Colorado.

5

Outdoor Growing Of Medical Marijuana And Recreational Pot- General Do And Don'ts

This book leans toward the *pros* of outdoor growing for yield purposes. The Californians have been growing outdoor crops for decades. The Californians did teach a lot of Coloradans how to grow marijuana. The truth is that a lot of California marijuana farmers have moved to Colorado. Some California medical marijuana farmers moved to Colorado during the medical marijuana boom. This was during the years of 2005-2008, and laws applying to dispensaries were almost non-existent during this period in Colorado.

All city and townships have government websites. The author can recommend areas to date, where outdoor growing is legal. Currently, on today's date, town and city website ordinances usually apply to medical mj dispensaries. They could have policies specifically directed to caregivers for plant counts in towns or city limits. Which does not do extended plant counts any good. So much medical mj is being grown in the city of Denver, that Denver now has an ordinance of a total of twelve plants per caregiver. The city of Denver and Denver County does not allow the growing of marijuana outdoors. This may or may not make town councils of surrounding suburbs of Denver decide the opposite when coming to the policy of outdoor growing. Some town councils may allow it to attract more people living in the community (revenue), and some may copy Denver's outdoor policy.

Colorado City and town websites change as time moves on. It is the caregiver's responsibility to stay on top of any changes that take place with Colorado local laws. One piece of advice that I can give: Call/contact the city or town attorney that you are growing in or plan on growing in. If in doubt, prepare a list of questions for your town or city attorney. Record your conversation and if asked, tell him you would like to remain anonymous. Let the recording and information be known to your personal attorney. An hour of advice per year with your personal medical mj attorney is good practice. You should always ask if any upcoming changes in the marijuana regulations exist that you should know about. The attorneys like your input also.

An outdoor grow may take a more strict policy when it comes to town and city ordinances, only time will tell. But in general, the policy for dispensaries and the caregiver is that as long as it is not visible from the road, it's okay.[10A] To date, county, city, and town ordinances in most cases do not have policies for caregivers on the issue of outdoor growing. That may or may not change. Counties, cities, and townships can change their policies every year. The outdoor growing by dispensaries is not common now but is becoming more common every year, for the reason of keeping costs down. Sometimes certain areas do not fall under a jurisdiction of a town or city and are considered in the county. For the caregiver, the recommended guideline is no visibility of medical mj plants from all property lines and having a greenhouse secures the fact of no visibility.[10A]

One way that the Californians were successful at keeping law enforcement off their backs in Humboldt and other notorious marijuana counties was by setting up in numbers. Bringing in their neighbors, they built up the neighborhood as a growing community. This sounds cozy, but you want to choose professional people who have been running other businesses for ten to twenty years. Some young people will make money and spend it fast because they have never had money before. Some kids party too much, etc.

Once the neighborhood is built up, law enforcement may need the National Guard to do a raid. Legal issues may be required at this level of enforcement, especially if no problems existed in the neighborhood. Another idea is to just set up in a remote country area where neighbors are far apart. Do your research, because some country areas, counties of Colorado are not medical marijuana friendly. This may change over time with the legalization of recreational pot. Let's reinforce that Colorado is now the largest producer of mj in the world. Bottom line: *It is the caregiver's responsibility to keep within local town, city, and county guidelines in the state of Colorado.*

DO AND DON'TS OF SELLING MARIJUANA

There is so much mj in Colorado that the feds are highly unlikely to bust someone for growing mj. But they would not hesitate to bust you for selling it. The feds go after farmers growing over one hundred pounds. Not just Mexican gangs but American citizens are greedy and grow large crops in the National Forest.

The feds do have their hands pretty full with convictions of sales of mj. The sale of two ounces or less has been decriminalized. Growing medical mj and recreational pot is the very *legal* part of legality in the Great State of Colorado. The sale of larger amounts of mj is very much illegal. 'Growing' and 'selling', note the key difference in the two verbs. There are different guidelines for dispensaries.

Under Amendment 64 and recreational pot, all home grows are not allowed to sell marijuana.

Under Colorado state regulations, a medical marijuana patient may purchase from a dispensary or a caregiver two ounces of medical mj per day. Under recreational pot, the Colorado state adult citizen may purchase from recreational pot store, one ounce or less. The MED (Marijuana Enforcement Division) is doing a bad job of enforcing these rules.

If for some reason you have between five pounds and one hundred pounds in your possession and you are driving, the local authorities would not have an option to give you a summons. They would be required to call in the federal agency and federal charges would be issued. Do not drive with large amounts of marijuana.

Even if you were growing six plants under Colorado's Amendment 64 of Recreational Pot and the three plants in flower you just harvested weighed in at over five pounds, *do not drive with it.* It is safer to do business from your house. The authorities would not be allowed on your property without a warrant. This means the authorities would have to present to a judge reasonable doubt that illegal activity occurred at your property location. Also, they would have to have the time and proof to build a case against you. Let's just say they do not have time to build cases and they do not spend money to build cases. Do *not* have plants visible from the road if you are growing outside. If authorities can get a photo of the plants without even stepping on the property, they may be able to persuade a judge for a warrant. Especially if they believe you have large amounts of plants. A photo of outdoor marijuana plants from the road of six plants would not be enough evidence for a judge to issue a warrant.

The State of Colorado only gets easy revenue from consumption of marijuana. Additional consultation can be given, by appointment, on your best options. Information is key in today's world. Having as much information as possible helps an individual make the best decisions.

6

Colorado Revenue And Consumption

Consumption of medical mj and recreational pot brings in huge amounts of revenue at the city, county, state, and federal level. Governments get their cut in many ways. Well before the legalization of recreational pot are the life-changing, Colorado driving drug charge of DUI, driving while under the influence of alcohol or drugs, DWAI, driving while ability impaired, and DUID, driving while under the influence of drugs. All are Colorado criminal charges that can be given by police officers for driving under the influence of marijuana.

This system has determined that the use of medical or recreational pot use within twenty minutes before driving is illegal based on cannabinoid levels in the blood. Although this system is not aggressively used yet, it will someday bring in the revenue that alcohol offenses do. It will also be a model for all other states to copy and bring in revenue for any other state that chooses to legalize mj under medical or recreational uses. The swab, I have been told, looks like a cotton q- tip or a water-testing strip used in testing water in pools or hot tubs. The swab, known as a chemical test, will be allowed by law to be used by a police officer to place in the mouth of a automobile driver if the officer has suspicion that the driver has used marijuana twenty minutes prior to getting behind the wheel of the automobile. Serious driving infractions exist if the 'chemical test is refused'. If this swab tests positive, the officer then has the right to take the driver to the station for a blood or urine test. The blood test will show cannabinoid levels in the blood, and if at all possible a urine test is recommended as it usually only shows if THC is present. THC's ability to show a presence in the body for thirty days is a defense in this example, where a blood sample shows exact cannabinoid level at the time of testing. Since this system is in the baby stages, the bar has been set high. The bar will get lower as revenue builds to supply the cost of testing blood, and the system can get through the walls of attorneys. Meanwhile, law enforcement officers of Colorado will have the ability to give drug- driving charges for too many cannabinoids in your blood stream. Driving under the influence of drugs can also mean too many oxycodone prescription pills before driving. It's whatever the blood test reveals.

What does government do with revenue? If the revenue consistently grows, which it usually does because the driving laws are mandated, the revenue goes back into the system. Why? Because state-run motor vehicle systems/ government systems are making money, just like a successful business. But the government is not supposed to be a business. It is supposed to be an instrument of the people to help the people.

What the American people do not realize is that the United States government has figured out how to make lots of money off the American people. They do not care if they scar your record and put you in a category of having a disease such as alcoholism or drug addiction. But this is only where the United States government makes part of its money. The United States government has become a huge money-making corporation via the businesses and the working Joe of today. DUI, DWAI, and DUID all have proven to bring in large amounts of revenue from state to state under different abbreviations. Colorado is about to have a whole bunch more revenue.

The cities of Colorado all have police authorities that can issue DUIs or DWAIs. Don't forget the county sheriff and the state trooper.

The state of Colorado gets sales tax from reported sales of mj in dispensaries. This sales tax includes an enforcement tax, and the total tax revenue brought in per month at the city and state levels is neck and neck with alcohol tax revenue. The medical marijuana dispensaries have to pay a one time-fee in state regulation licenses of $60,000.00 to $100,000.00 just to open doors. This does not include the retail license costs for recreational pot sales, which is in addition to the prior dollar amount. This does not include overhead costs of buildings, utilities, labor, etc. Dispensaries have the option to spend more on additional state regulation licenses for an edible license, also referred to as an Infused Products Business, which allows the dispensary to have a commercial kitchen to cook edibles and make other bi-products such as hash oils. An OPC or Optional Premises Cultivation License can also be purchased by the Medical Marijuana Dispensary. The OPC can be purchased for several growing locations as long as all documentation is submitted to the state of Colorado and approved.   As of January 1, 2014, the dispensaries have the opportunity to purchase the recreational pot retail licenses, which can start at an additional $60,000.00.   There are also cultivation, infusion, and testing licenses for recreational pot. These regulation licenses are transferable if the dispensary is sold, given the dispensary has no outstanding violations, and the potential new owner of the dispensary has had a Colorado drivers license for at least two years with no felony criminal record.

7

Growing Marijuana In Colorado, Media, And Preparing A Home For Marijuana.

The author has used every medium known. He does have a preference and will try to give an opinion of plus and minus on all media.

The author will touch briefly on the trends of the dispensary and how the dispensary should be looked at in the mj industry as the corporation. The big dispensaries are growing more mj than anyone in the world and they have the highest costs. That being said, the price of mj has dropped considerably in the past seven to eight years. Recreational pot has created another boom increasing prices recently. The price of marijuana goes up and down based on the supply and demand. It generally has its highest value during the months of August and September.

These months are the months right before outdoor harvest. Outdoor harvests do affect the price of marijuana whether the marijuana is legally grown or not. At outdoor harvest, supply is at its highest and price at its lowest. The two months before harvest can see the lack of supply and more demand. Large marijuana farmers have been known to hold on to their inventories and only sell when the demand and price is high. Outdoor crops are so significant in volume that they can affect the price of marijuana all through the course of a year. Most farmers will sell any inventory in the months of August and September regardless, to make space for the fall harvest inventory. The holidays of Thanksgiving and Christmas usually show an increase in price for marijuana regardless of supply and demand.

A considerable profit can still be made, but only a cost-conscious mj farmer would make more money. The dispensaries have large overhead costs, commercial buildings, utilities, employee payroll, etc.

Which kinds of mj do not need anything but water to flourish? The dispensaries know, because they have been running specific strains side by side. *Golden Goat* is a strain/type of medical marijuana. For example, two plants of the same strain are put side by side and of the same size and health. One Golden Goat mj plant has as many nutrients as you can spend on the damn plant. Then another golden goat mj plant has just treated water. That's how a farmer is able to determine if a strain of mj can live with just water alone and maximize yield just as well as the plant that had two hundred dollars in premium fertilizers its entire life. Trial and error is the method used.

The dispensaries are trying to cut costs by using expensive lighting. These new state-of-the-art lights are high-pressure sodium, and go up to 1000watt, but do not put out heat. This saves in costs of cooling and ventilation. The new state-of-the-art lights have an incentive for you to purchase because the energy/electric company offers rebates on the new purchase of these lights. They are made by a well-known manufacturer, but are not mass-produced yet.

A medical mj dispensary owner is technically a caregiver or a partnership of two or more caregivers. State regulations do not allow for caregivers to partnership in a business format unless they have applied for and are approved by the state of Colorado to purchase a medical mj dispensary license or grow facility license. Currently, new dispensary licenses are not being issued by the state of Colorado. A medical mj dispensary license may be transferred by a current owner of a license even if the actual business building is no longer available (example, the lease did not get renewed).

Caregivers can learn from the dispensary when it comes to business practices. Now that you can see some of the ways that the big guys cut costs and why they try to cut costs, you will see why the author is a fan of outdoor farming of mj. The techniques and qualities of outdoor mj in Colorado have been so good for so long that it almost looks like indoor grown mj, and it can also be sold for the same price as indoor grown mj. With considerable cost savings in mind, we will move forward in medias pros and cons.

MEDIA

No Colorado regulations or laws restrict a caregiver from growing medical marijuana at his home.

Let's make some baby mj plants. I would like to start with media first, because I like to have a home for my babies before I make the babies. For beginners, you can get a feel for how much work you are getting into. Once you have an assembly line, it will not be as much work. Gardening is repetitious and therapeutic. If you get tired of talking to people, then farming may be for you. Plants all have different personalities like people, but they don't talk.

My preferred medium is a blend of peat (peat is mainly for better flavor in the taste of medical mj), perlite, cocoa, humus, and I do amend or condition with bat guano, chicken manure, worm castings, and cow manure. I will only use treated water. I often substitute pea gravel for the perlite because it is very inexpensive. This teaching tip is for outdoor farmers who are using containers. Your medical mj plants can get twenty times bigger when using a plant container versus putting them in the ground, in Colorado's short outdoor growing season. The reason being that you will be feeding them in a hydroponic manner. In the ground, they tend to need less water (nutrient solution) in spring and fall, when it can be cooler.

When farming from pots or containers, high winds may knock plants over when the plants get large. To avoid that, put an inch to two inches of pea gravel in the bottom of the pot/ container. This gives the pot weight so the plant will not get knocked over from wind. This mix recipe is for your big pots that you will make your final transplant into. Raised beds are a good option, but I find that if you're in a small area you can squeeze more plants into an area with pots. Pots will be a little more work, but more medicine hitting the scale.

For your baby plants, start with a *solo* plastic cup, which can be found at grocery stores. Prepare these cups by just taking a knife and making an incision on the bottom for drainage.

No nutrients/fertilizers for baby plants. The rule of thumb for plants in general is no fertilizer until they are a foot tall or bigger. That means none in the dirt and none in the water. Only cocoa, peat, and perlite for the solo plastic cups.

Although it is not necessary, I like to transplant to a second size before going to my last and very large pot. From the solo plastic cup, I like to go to a three-gallon pot or just smaller than a three-gallon pot. The three- gallon pot will have cocoa, perlite, peat, and one/half teaspoon of bat guano, and one/half teaspoon chicken manure. The reason I use three gallon pots is because some spring seasons can be colder than others and depending on the farmers' almanac, I will set up my little green house for the spring.

I have been known to take an entire year to sell my whole medicine- bud inventory. Some years it sells in six to eight months. If I am out of MMJ buds in the spring when I start a new crop, I have been known to my friends as the Home Depot of plants. Selling baby plants for sixty dollars and large plants for $160.00. I had one guy rent a *U-haul,* fourteen-foot box truck so he could pick up some big plants. Plants can bring in extra spending money if you are out of bud medicine, MMJ inventory for sales.

Growing more than you intend to 'run' in your final crop allows for two things. (1) A little extra pocket money from plant sales, (2) but most importantly, it gives you the flexibility to go through your herd and cut down any weak or struggling. A lot of farmers fail to do this and spend money and labor on plants that will not yield like the

others. Keep in mind the ultimate number your goal is from beginning to end. *Also keep in mind the federal guideline of ninety-nine plants
or less.* Regardless, you will get a feel for what one man is capable of.

Either outdoor or indoor, the author chooses dirt as a medium. This
can still be referred to as a hydroponic system. By only using treated
water, I use a flood delivery system along with what I like to call inducers (early flowering products) to speed the duration of the crop. These
inducers/early flowering products will be listed in another chapter.

A hydroponic system with the use of only Hydrotin, or pea gravel,
or rock wool cubes as media, would not be sustainable in an outdoor
system unless in a greenhouse that has a controlled environment
similar to an indoor grow set up. The reason is between heat and
evaporation and plant uptake of water, it would not be cost effective
and the use of green houses is an additional overhead cost.

The cocoa coir medium has pros and cons. Let's start with the
pros. I like the use of little cocoa pucks for seeds. These look like the
size of vanilla wafer cookies. Once hydrated, they can be the size of a
cardboard toilet paper roll to half and third that size. These shapes
and sizes usually have a cheesecloth type wrapping around them to
keep the cocoa in a certain puck shape. These can be good as long
as they have good ventilation and drainage.

Cocoa is a neutral medium in the sense that it has no acidity or
base qualities. Technically, it could be used as a PH filter, but if in
doubt check your PH going into the medium and check your PH
going out of the medium. Checking PH should be done any time fertilizers or a nutrient is added to the water-feeding solution. Medical
mj likes a PH of six point zero to five point eight.

The price of marijuana used to be much higher, allowing for the
higher expense account for growing. During the first marijuana
boom in Colorado, experimentation not only saw the use of liquid
nutrients used to get the plants the size of *rhinos*, but nutrients were
overused, causing plant burning and nutrient lockout. The price of
MMJ medicine coming down has actually led to a closer-to-organic

product, because less ingredients are being flushed through plants and genetics are relied on as a priority.

One of the big pluses to cocoa is the time and money saved on the correction of PH on your nutrient solution. If cocoa coir is not being used as fifty percent of the medium, then nutrient solutions added to the pot need to be PH corrected, especially if you are using a lot of liquid nutrients. The mj plants will thank you and the chances of burning are less likely. The coca coir having excellent PH qualities is recommended as part of the blend for all media.

Flushing is the practice of running water through the plant medium and is primarily used to rid the medium and the *plant* of unwanted residuals and chemicals.

If cocoa coir is used one hundred percent as the medium, problems with salt build up could occur. Salt can show its visual sign of white residue forming on the surface area of the cocoa at the top of the container where nutrients are added. If cocoa coir is used as the primary medium then extra flushing between feeds could be necessary for plants to stay healthy. Smaller plants will not hold up to salt build up as well as the bigger plants do. Extra flushing could result in more water costs and labor.

I like a blend of peat and cocoa in my large pots, all the way to the small solo plastic cups. Peat can be acidic. Using cocoa as a blend counters the acidity of peat. The overall consensus in Colorado is the use of dirt products used more so than any other medium. I have seen others so impressed with the size of my plants that they switched from a RO (reverse osmosis) hydroponic system to dirt just for size reasons. The main reason I was taught to use a dirt medium by my teachers is because fewer things can go wrong, making it a little easier. Another main reason is because most people notice better flavor in the medical mj when smoked. You can disagree with my opinion, but the trend in Colorado is dirt.

Another trend building in Colorado is the use of Koi or tilapia fish-ponds or tanks to fertilize the plants. They can also be used as a reservoir to an indoor hydroponic system.

This 350-gallon tank is being used for water storage. When farming a large crop, water back up is not necessary, but you never know when a water shortage may be a threat. This tank 'top' can be removed with a reciprocating saw. It can also be used as a reservoir for 'tilapia' fish.

These systems can be recommended as a drip system. The nutrients from fish droppings and the water that fish live in can be beneficial and organic to the plant, especially in the flower stage. Tilapia can also be eaten. Especially if the fish get big enough they are outgrowing their home.

8

Indoor Growing Rooms for the Beginner, Clones and Cloning, Preparing Baby Containers for Clones, Seeds and Seedlings, Seed versus Clone, Dips.

Now that we have a medium selected, you will need a couple small indoor rooms in order to maximize yield. Start inside. (This is where extended plant counts come in to play. If you have the acreage, you could start outside later and have higher plant counts/ less plants started inside. Smaller plants in higher plant numbers equal a crop of big plants in lower plant numbers. Whether you have acreage or not, starting inside will maximize yield outdoors.)

In Colorado, the outdoor growing season can be shorter than other parts of the USA. By having the indoor rooms you have a controlled environment to start your mj baby plants. If you are intending on growing mj as a living, you would need at least one to two grow rooms for outdoor growing and three grow rooms for indoor growing. Even most dispensary owners have grow rooms at home. If they do not, then they are relying on another farmer to grow their mj.

People may not realize that growing medical mj makes them a farmer. Farming takes a green thumb, but it's also a type of work that involves repetition much like other skilled work. It can be considered a trade much like carpentry, masonry, or even fishing or logging. All of these trades have secrets to them. This book allows you to make decisions of a ten-year veteran farmer of medical marijuana. The list of products I have prepared in chapter thirteen, will make farming medical mj very satisfying, year after year.

For *outdoor* growing, a person could probably get away with just one indoor grow room, but two would be ideal if you are planning on moving your business in a growing direction. 1) A closet in a corner of small room for clones. 2) One vegetative room. Also if you have your indoor vegetative room adjacent to your outdoor growing area, it will involve less labor moving things around.

Many *indoor* set ups should consider: 1. A room or closet for cloning and or seedlings or both. This room will also have to be big enough for your female mother plant that you will be taking your cuttings from for clones. *But* an entire separate room for mothers is suggested, we will call this 2. The vegetative room. The veg room should be big enough to have several plants. The reason being that if you are taking cuttings from female mother plants, then you want to choose cuttings from the strongest, healthiest plants. Some plants of the same strain of medical mj may even have stronger odor than another.

It is wise to grow a couple or several kinds of medical mj. In Colorado, so many kinds of medical mj exist that it can be hard to satisfy the patient with one specific strain. Sell or give away female mothers that are second in size and overall characteristics. By cloning you are taking cells from one plant and making an identical plant with the same cells. 3. The flower room is for what is called twelve-twelve lighting and usually will have 600watt to 1000watt lights, which requires ventilation due to very high heat temperatures.

This property addition made outdoor farming easier and improved annual income. It also helped property resell for 60% above market value. Photos as illustrations will show how the author has improved residential properties to make 'work from home' incomes and improve property resale.

4. A trimming room should be considered, as well as 5. A drying room.

Indoor grows should be set up so every room is full at all times of the year. Once a harvest takes place, the veg plants are brought into the flower room. Clones are brought into the vegetative room, and cuttings are taken for new baby clones. This constant rotation ensures that when you are done trimming, it will be close to harvest time again. It also secures year-round income with year round work.

For the outdoor grow, I have been known to use the vegetative room as the dry room. For the outdoor grow, the steps are clone room, veg room, outdoors, and back to veg room for drying. Using the veg room as the drying room saves for the need of a fifth room.

With an outdoor crop, instead of year-round work, you can try to get a month or two off. The outdoor crop will be larger than the indoor crops combined. It is a different mind set. But works regardless.

CLONES and the choices involved.

The first thing you will need is a fluorescent light, specifically a fluorescent T5. For beginners, you will want to consider three fluorescent lights. One for cloning, and two for the vegetative room. We will call the Fluorescents T5s. The T5 light with eight light bulbs, called a *quantum badboy* can be found for sale on many Internet sources. These lights will last a lifetime. I prefer blue bulbs. Blue light is a bit brighter, and if you are growing from seed, blue light can stimulate a seedling to having a female sex by just a slightly better chance than a male plant. Although T5s put out heat, they do not put out as much heat as a 1000 watt light. Beginners *may not* get a feel for what problems heat will cause, with just T5s. Most times, T5s put out just enough heat to maintain ideal room temperature. It really depends on the time of year. Winter may call for an additional heater with T5s. In summer, use extra fans with windows open, possibly max fan

Pictured are small plants soon to be going outdoors. This garage has 10-foot high ceilings for plenty of space for tall indoor plants in the winter season. This garage also provides plant-drying space for the outdoor crop.

This space does not have the drying equipment in place.
The picture shows strings suspended from the ceiling joists with yellow markers.
When drying plants, the plants can be hung from the ceiling and then a
second course below that at the ends of the strings.

ventilation. Without the use of proper ventilation, heat and moisture can cause condensation on windows and walls. This condensation can cause powdery mildew. We will refer to powdery mildew as PM. A medical mj plant can't tolerate PM on its own. Powdery mildew sprays will be addressed in a later chapter. Your best defense against PM is proper ventilation and a clean growing room.

When preparing for clones and seedlings there are many ways to skin a cat. Deciding how you will utilize your grow space really should not be a quick decision. In Colorado, see grow rooms first hand before constructing your own. When I first became a caregiver, I had the opportunity to see a lot of grow rooms. Not one is identical, but most are very similar (example, clone area, veg room, flower room, ventilation, etc.). If everyone is doing things very similar, then there is a system. Call ahead before visiting different dispensaries in Colorado. Very many of them have at least one grow room visible to the public. Look at as many set ups as you can before you build your own.

Although these preparations are not completely necessary, they do make cleaning easier. Even though you are only starting clones and seedlings, the preparation of the room should be a one-time deal in order to save time and money. Most growers either make changes as they go, *or* add remodel upgrades to grow rooms when the money to remodel is available. 1. Concrete floors are preferable with a drain. Basements have always been traditionally good growing areas. Basements are hard to find with ten -foot high ceilings.

Warehouses can insure that you will have space for *rhino* sized plants. If you do not have concrete floors then a Shop Vacuum is a *must*. A shop vacuum is a tool every marijuana farmer owns. Shop vacuums are useful from beginning to end in a farmer's tool arsenal. 2. Your walls are going to have to be reflective in order to be productive in plant growth. I prefer concrete walls because they can be painted a glossy white and cleaned easier than other surfaces. If concrete is not an option other surfaces will do. Keep in mind that white

There's no floor drains on this concrete floor.
The two garage doors allow for easy spray out with hose.

has been proven to be equally as reflective as other reflective colored materials. White is the main choice in Colorado because you can see if it is dirty and needs to be cleaned or re-painted. The plastic rolls of white poly or reflective poly work well. You want to install them as flat as possible in order to be effective. The wall surface should be clean and cleanable, because insects and PM can get between the reflective material and the wall. This is why ready-made tents or closets sell well in magazines and Internet. If your grow-room walls do not allow for reflective paint or materials, an additional overhead grow light can be the solution. 3. Ventilation should be used in the form of an in-line duct fan or *can fan*. Odor is generally not an issue in the vegetative stage. When in the flower stage, a carbon *can* and inline canister fan should work, depending on how close to neighbors your location is.

One thousand watt light hoods have fittings for your six to eight inch ventilation ducting. Fluorescents generally do not. If you need ventilation for your T5s, you can run your ventilation ducting high along the ceiling where your heat will rise first. Just run the open end of duct vent pipe close to the T5s and it will work fine. Fireplace stacks and wood stoves, if not being used as a heat source, can be an easy place to put your can fan and exhaust the heat through the fireplace stack. You may have to cut a custom hole in the wall to run your vent pipe out of. *Keep in mind*: this exhaust fan could have some noise like your kitchen cooking-range exhaust fan. If you have a *nosey* neighbor, it's best to put this exhaust out a wall that is not blowing to a neighbor. Also be aware of the constant noise it may make. Sometimes a nosey neighbor will pay attention if he hears a fan noise constantly. If coming out of fireplace stack, it is usually up high enough that the wind takes the noise and odor up high above households.

Even though mj is legal in Colorado not everyone likes it. Set up a grow like it is still highly illegal. Do not let neighbors know you are growing and do not unload truckloads of grow supply that can be seen by the neighbors. I have been known to work at night so neighbors can't see what I'm carrying into the house. Keep up with any new regulations made by the state of Colorado every upcoming new-year. Although the state of Colorado has been unsuccessful in the past, they have tried to make the 1000-foot *no*-drug distance apply to city parks also.

The room layout for your clones and vegetative area should not need remodeling by an electrician. The use of T5s can be used on regular 120V outlets. But if you have the money, you may want to have additional outlets for oscillating fans. These are necessary to produce air movement for the plants to simulate natural wind. Plants need movement by air for their leaves and flex branches. This creates the stimulation of plant hormones that cause growth. These are all things to consider in business start-up costs. If an electrical remodel does take place, make sure it is by a journeyman electrician who does all work to building code.

CLONES AND CLONING

Lets start with a clone closet the size of one T5. Now, you can purchase a pre-made closet, but I am a very tall man, and never had an interest in working in a tent. Although a closet is not necessary, it can help you control the climate and temperature. Cloning can be frustrating, but once you get good at it, you will be well on your way to mastering the basics of medical marijuana farming. Cloning should be the area of farming medical marijuana that you concentrate on the most. Everything else will come easy once you have success at cloning. The top three teaching tips that helped me are, (1) *Light*, (2) *Temperature*, (3) *Strains* of mj that genetically root easily.

I would not waste your time with a light of anything less than a fluorescent T5. The light used for cloning would be light *on* twenty-four hours around the clock. Once you have the light, then you can plan your closet design. A clone machine can be used, but for beginners I recommend rock wool cubes and a propagation bubble. Your budget may not be huge starting out. They both work and I run large crops with both tools.

A clone closet can be constructed in the corner of a room to save space. Keep in mind the T5 will be above and at the top of your closet.

I use scrap two by four stud lumber for the corners, and braces the length of the T5. You do not have to be a carpenter to do this project. One/half inch plywood can be used to make your table platform that you will be resting your propagation bubbles on. Make your platform table at a height you will be working from in a chair or standing. Make sure to keep the table at a distance that the propagation bubble is eight inches away from the light or less. *Some* T5 lights put out more heat than others. Some T5 lights do not put out as much heat, and can be put directly on plant surfaces.

Once your framing work is completed, you can run cross braces along the top and fasten hooks to hang your T5. Choose either reflective or white plastic poly to wrap your closet with. A hand staple-gun can be used to fasten pieces on three sides of closet. Use thumbtacks on the fourth side that you will be entering for working. Turn on the light in the closet with a small standing office desk fan at one end. Let the light and fan run for twenty-four to forty-eight hours.

You can never have enough thermometers in this business. I like to put two digital thermometers of different brands in my closet. This way I can take the average temperature of the two, or I can take the info from the one I think is more accurate. I have so many that I can tell you that even the same name-brand thermometer can read a different temperature.

The most ideal temperature for root growth is between seventy-eight and eighty-two degrees Fahrenheit. This should be one of the biggest rules to follow as a beginner and a seasoned pro. Heat pads with thermostats can be purchased for your tabletop. These are not necessary based on cabinet temperature. Heat pads work and I advise them if a cabinet is not an option. The use of the cabinet is to insure ample light and constant temperature. After the clone closet T5 and fan have been on for twenty-four to forty-eight hours, we can assume this will be the average temperature before we modify the clone closet.

If it is too cool, you can try turning off the fan with just the T5 light on. If it is too hot you can try opening a piece of the reflective poly at one corner behind the fan, or at the other end of closet where hot air can blow out easier, or both. Get your clone closet at the proper temperature before you start cutting up a mother mj plant.

Let's move to rock wool cubes. You will need as many rock wool cubes as the number of plants you are planning to grow. I generally like to have an extra amount in case of failure. If you have more clones than you can use, you will find you can usually sell or trade them. You can give them away, but try never to kill mj plants unless they are weak, diseased, or have bugs.

I like to use a large mixing bowl or clean five-gallon bucket. I use treated water, which means go to a pet store and get a water treatment for fish-tank water. This will neutralize chlorine and other heavy metals. You will also need an inexpensive PH tester, which can be found at grow stores.

Once you have your water PH neutral and treated, add your rock wool cubes to soak for twenty-for hours. Test your PH one more time after rock wool has soaked. It should test five-point-eight to six–point-zero on the PH test. I like to store my treated water in clean, one-gallon jugs. You should not need too much treated water when cloning. Also have a new spray bottle with treated water. Clones like to be misted and in a humid climate when they are babies.

Once you have your rock wool soaking, you will have to choose a rooting hormone. I have tried most of them. They are all made up of slightly different ingredients, *but they all work*. A trace amount of the hormone can be added to your water that the rock wool is soaking in. The biggest tip I can give you and the one thing that helped with my cloning is a product made by *General Hydroponics* called *Rapid Start*. This can be added to your rock-wool soaking solution only at fifty-percent strength of what is recommended on the bottle as a nutrient solution mix. These rock wool cubes *do not* need to be saturated and dripping water for hours on end after they are soaked for twenty-four hours.

Take a clean porcelain dinner plate and set six prepped rock wool cubes on one side of the plate. Once the excess water has run on to the plate for five minutes, your rock wool cube is ready for a cutting.

The first teaching tip for cuttings from a mother mj plant is to know where to cut to have a better success rate. I am pretty anal about grooming my plants. I like to groom my mother plants about a month before I take cuttings. Don't over do it. Go in the bottom and middle of the plant and thin branches and leaves that are weak or have been shaded by large branches above. Again, don't over do it, because the strong lower branches are the best spot to take your cuttings. The mother plant will be defined from grooming and you will know exactly where you are going to cut on cutting day.

Also, turning the pot of vegetative plants under artificial and natural sunlight allows for the plant to get bright light on all sides. A one-third turn to half turn every two weeks to a month. Of course turning small plants is easier than turning big plants. You can turn small plants much more often. This practice results in maximum yield.

The hormones at the bottom and middle of a plant are the best place to take cuttings. Have a glass of treated water prepared before taking your cuttings. Try to have as little as possible time for the actual cut area to be exposed to air before putting it in your cup of treated water. Only take about six cuts at a time, so you can go to your root hormone and rock wool. Cutting the very ends of branches is the best location for a cutting. Be sure to use a new razor that has been cleaned with alcohol prior to use.

The ideology of cuttings is to take them the size of two to three inches in height with not too many leaves and branches. The process of cutting and growing roots will be the most stressful parts of the clone lifeline. When a cutting first sprouts roots, it is supporting all the leaves on that cutting. So too many leaves on a cutting can cause additional stress. There is a fine line between too many leaves and not enough. I like to allow for trimming two to three yellowing leaves off the cutting in the seven to ten days it's trying to pop roots. During a seven to ten day period, some leaves may yellow. These should be trimmed off on a daily basis, because the yellow leaves can mildew if not removed. Mildew is not your friend.

Start an assembly line. Have your rooting hormone prepared on a clean porcelain saucer along with another clean plate of prepped rock wool cubes. Take your cutting from the glass of treated water and cut the stem four inches in length. Then at the bottom of your stem, cut the stem at a diagonal. Try to do this in a timely manner to avoid the cut edge of stem being exposed to the air. Only place the cut portion along the diagonal into the rooting hormone. Expose the cut to the hormone recommended on your directions on your choice of rooting hormone, usually ten seconds. Insert the cutting into your rock wool cube about one half inch to an inch. Instead of inserting the cutting directly into the center of the rock wool cube, I like to insert just off of center. This allows for visibility of roots a little sooner for managing strong clones to transplant. I will prep about six clones at a time and carry over to my closet on a clean plate and place in the already climatic-propagation bubble/tray.

I like to keep track of different types of medical mj strains. And also manage first/strong root poppers from late root poppers. I take the strongest for myself. I keep track of different kinds of medical mj in a couple different ways once it is in a rock wool cube. (1) You can use separate propagation bubbles and mark with black marker, GG Golden Goat a Colorado strain. If the different propagation bubbles are going to take up too much space in your closet? (2) Then you may want to go to the hardware store and buy colored plastic zip ties. Cut these colored zip ties up into one - two inch lengths and insert into the rock wool cubes. Yellow for Golden Goat, red for Jump-in-jack-flash, etc. The key is never to use markers on the inside of your humid propagation bubble, such as wood toothpicks that can mold. (3) You could divide your propagation bubble in to one/half, one/third, one/ quarter and simply just draw a diagram of what strain is in what quarter of the propagation bubble. I have been known to squeeze forty to fifty clones in one propagation bubble.

When using a cloning machine, you want to have a strong closet to support the weight of the water. A closet is not necessary for this machine but I recommend the lid and a good T5. Most cloning machines are used on a floor with chain-link extending the T5 down to the machine. The same practice of running this machine with the light on for thirty-six hours is a good idea. It may take your water temperature that long to adjust to room temperature, and give you a desired temperature. Check your water temperature before taking cuttings. Remember your ideal cloning temperature is seventy-eight degrees to eighty-two degrees F. These machines are going to save you some time. I cannot say that they are any better than rock wool. If using a cloning machine, try to use a machine that is the size that will produce half the amount of the total crop number you need. You can do two runs with the machine to total the entire numbers you need for your planned crop. Your rooting hormone of choice will have directions for the mix, for the clone machines. You can also use *General Hydroponics, Rapid Start* at half strength in your machine nutrients. I notice a positive difference with this product.

The internal PVC plumbing can be replaced easily. Once you have enough time on the machine, you will have algae build up on the inside of the PVC plumbing. I prefer peroxide to bleach as a cleaner for this machine. I also use isopropyl alcohol as a wipe down once the machine is clean. This is an attempt to kill any cells of algae that may remain. I do a final wipe down with tap water. Alcohol may be overkill to an already good cleaner of peroxide. Keeping your indoor and outdoor grow as clean as possible is a good repetition. A cleaning checklist is good to have for a weekly basis. A list will be recommended in chapter sixteen.

Although the store-bought clone machines can be very expensive and out of sight for a beginner's budget, if you take a close look at how the display model looks, you can build an inexpensive one. The parts for these machines are about one/half to one/third of the new machine. Your labor can be cheap. A clean plastic container with lid can substitute as the machine body. Make sure to use a dark color or

This is a cloning machine. The MK stands for MK Ultra and it's a very
dense medical marijuana strain. Most cloning machines have a considerable
cost and usually are not in the budget of a beginner marijuana farmer.)

paint the plastic container black. You do not want your roots getting light in any situation possible. Take a photo with your cell phone of the store display machine, so you can figure the budget on the parts. The plastic container can be of the storage chest style.

PREPARING BABY CONTAINERS FOR CLONES, SEEDS, AND SEEDLINGS

The solo plastic cups should be clean and new, run after run. These will be baby containers for your newly rooted clones. I like to pre-pare these before I start my cuttings and rock wool. The preparation should consist of your drain holes, dirt of your choice, and wetting the dirt. Once the dirt is wet in the cups, place the cups in a box and place in a warm room so the dirt is at the ideal rooting temperature of seventy-eight to eighty-two degrees F. At this point your rock wool clones have a home to go to.

Use the *General Hydroponics Rapid Start* at fifty-percent strength in your wetting solution for the solo plastic cups. *Rapid Start* can be used through the entire vegetative stage. If you are on a budget, it is better used sooner than later. I like to concentrate on roots first and foremost with clones and seedlings. Common sense says you cannot have a big plant without big roots. The plastic solo cups should be of the darkest color possible. You want no light getting through to the roots. Never use a clear plastic cup.

These solo plastic cups are great for marking notes on the cup with a magic marker. I will write the strain type and mark First Crop on clones that are the healthiest. By writing notes on your plastic cups, you can manage your crop one hundred percent. First crop gets the best real estate. What is meant by first crop is when the plant is three feet tall, if it still appears to be superior to the second crop then I will give the first crop the best sunlight and biggest pots. Most of the time second crop can and does catch up to first crop within two to three weeks. You will find yourself giving your best real estate to a certain strain of medical mj over others.

When the clones are still inside under artificial light, I tend to put the strongest ones out on the edge of the light and give the weaker clones the most direct light in order to try to let them catch up to the strong ones. When your propagation bubbles start to get empty, you can combine clones into one or two propagation bubbles and make room in your closet for the solo plastic cups. This being said, keep in mind your closet table should be strong enough to hold wet solo cups full of dirt.

When transplanting your rock-wool-rooted clone to your solo cups, leave some space–an inch from the top, so you have room to transplant a rock wool cube and rooted clone in the cup. I like to have these cups prepped and up to the desirable temperature of seventy-eight to eighty- two degrees F, before I transplant rock wool and clones to the cup.

I find that the best tool to wet your dirt in your plastic solo cups is with a bicycle water bottle. This bottle has a nipple that lets you control the nutrient solution going into the cup better without splashing and making much less mess. When transplanting your rock wool and clone to the cup, I prefer the dirt on the wetter side because it is more forgiving to roots' snapping and breaking when transplanting rock wool to the cup. The same holds true for clones coming out of a cloning machine without rock wool. These are babies, be gentle.

As a general rule, do not over water. For the transition of rock wool to solo plastic cup, I have the dirt pretty wet for transplanting and the clones are used to a humid environment from the propagation bubble. You can cut back on dirt wetness once the transplant is complete and force the roots to grow to the bottom of the cup by trying to have the moisture at the bottom of the cup. This can be achieved by putting your cups in a tray and feeding from the bottom. This is done by putting the nutrient solution in the tray and letting the drain holes in the cup allow water in the bottom. When I mention nutrient solution, keep in mind this is just *Rapid Start* and treated water. No fertilizer until the plants are twelve inches or bigger.

The best rule of thumb for watering clones in plastic solo cups and small vegetative plants in pots is to lift the solo plastic cup. If it is light in weight, water it. If it is heavy then it has enough moisture. Never stick your fingers in the dirt to determine if there is enough moisture in the dirt medium. *A common mistake by beginner farmers is over watering* and yellowing is a sign of a potentially dead baby clones.

If you do not already have a fan in your clone closet, put one at one end. The fan is very much necessary to help the clones get stronger. The fan simulates natural wind movement that would flex and move branches and leaves. This plant movement stimulates the plants' hormones and the hormones make the plant grow bigger. Put the strong clones up by the fan that can handle the stronger air movement and the weaker clones on the opposite end of the fan. Once you can see the weaker clones catching up, rotate them closer to the fan where the air movement is strong.

Clones and vegetative plants like a cool mist. Prepare a new clean spray bottle with treated water only. Spray clones in a propagation bubble often. Once the clones are in plastic solo cups, use the hand sprayer and cool mist often. Once the plants are large and outside, use a large sprayer for cool misting. A two to three gallon sprayer marked with magic marker H20. Do not to spray water for cool misting in direct sun light. Cool misting outdoors should be done before eight AM and just before dark. Some strains may not like cool misting and this is another reason to label all plants and keep strains organized for best management. Cool misting can also be referred to as foliar feeding. Foliar feeding means feeding by rainfall or trying to reproduce a natural rainfall in a man-made feed from up above. I do not recommend anything but treated water for foliar feeding. Some strains are sensitive to foliar feed and only like to be fed from the roots. This is where a journal is very useful for memory over the years. Foliar feeding with treated water gives the plant small amounts of Nitrogen. Cool misting can be a good indicator as to whether you have a flying bug problem.

The one-gallon sprayer can be used for early morning
cool misting during vegetative plant stage.

Flying bugs do not like the moisture of cool misting. White flies and flies generally live under leaves to stay cool. Both do not like the moisture of cool misting. If you see bugs flying out and away from plants when cool misting, then you have irritated the flying bugs and possibly, white flies. White flies increase in numbers if you do not control them. Yellow sticky traps should be used first. Whiteflies are tiny and white, but can live on leaves, causing the leaves to be less productive, decreasing maximum yield. Leaves can get white, yellow, or brown speckles if white flies are to the point of infestation.

SEEDS AND SEEDLINGS/ SEED VERSUS CLONE

The main reasons a portion of a marijuana crop would be grown from a seed is because a seed plant will have a slightly better flavor. First- generation clones from the sexed female mothers can also be valuable for flavor and aroma reasons. In general, seed plants can be slightly stronger, and will need very little supports from lattice or bamboo supports, even when heavy with buds. The introduction of a strain of medical mj by seed can be considered a pure and truly disease-and-pest- free plant. These reasons may or may not outweigh the reasons for using a clone. Seedlings can be a little more work, because they have to be sexed. A couple of different ways exist for a seed plant can be sexed. Male plants with seeds can't be used for sale of smokable medical mj and there is no market for medical mj with seeds.

Growing an entire crop from seed would show a farmer that seed plants can vary in size and yield even if the same seeds are used from one individual medical mj strain. Medical mj is very sensitive to light and clones can have seeds if they do not get correct lighting. Lighting of all types and situations will be discussed in chapter fourteen.

A marijuana farmer may or may not be able to get more money for a crop grown from seed that has more flavor. The reason for grow-ing would be more for the having very tasty medicine for the farmers' personal head/medicine stash. Clones cut from a female seedling

Purps is a very tasty strain of medical marijuana.

plant would have great value to a medical mj farmer. These would be considered first-generation clones and have the reputation of having more aroma and flavor of a clone that was tenth generation. Having seeds and a seed bank gives a medical mj farmer more depth on how to run his crop. By having a seed bank, a farmer does not have to rely on other medical mj farmers or dispensaries for clones.

Preparing female plants from seed for the intentions of first-generation female clones is considerable work, but this is the closest way to organic farming known. Although starting out to close to one-hundred-percent organic with seed, without expensive testing, there is no way of knowing if the plant the seed came from was somehow exposed to inorganic substances. Organic versus inorganic will be discussed in chapter eleven. I and many other farmers believe that there is no such thing as one-hundred-percent organic. You can only try to be close to one- hundred-percent organic by certain practices. You may or may not be able to get to a harvest of medical mj without using non- organic products to get your investment to sale. There are ethics involved with some inorganic products. If they are used properly, they are safe according to the manufacturers.

Let's reinforce that clones are the identical cells taken from a healthy strong female plant. Seeds can give a medical mj farmer peace of mind in that a seedling is a virgin in the sense it has no powdery mildew or bugs or any other known diseases unless your grow room or farm is dirty and already has or had one of the above. Bringing clones onto your property by purchase from another medical mj farmer or a dispensary always leaves you at risk of bringing something into your grow room or farm. Clones are a form of host that can carry bugs, powdery mildew, etc. Other hosts are dogs, people, etc.

Male plants can pollenate an entire female farm. People have been known to try to sabotage medical mj farms with a male plant. I was victim of this sabotage twice. But I had good inspection practices on a daily basis and noticed male plants and got them off the farm immediately before they could pollenate the entire crop. Marijuana farmers can pretend to be your friend and then slip you a male plant. If they sabotage your crop they make theirs more valuable. Outside of sabotage, a male plant can be brought by the mistake of any human.

Sexing seed plants is work. Once you have sexed a seed plant and know it's a female, grow that female seed plant/ seedling as big as you can and see if it is worth cloning in the vegetative stage. Beginners need to focus on all factors of keeping buds seedless. Getting reputable clones is luck sometimes. All you can really do is take a look at different farms and dispensaries, see the quality of how they are run/managed, and offer to pay for the clones. Large amounts of clones should get you a better price per clone. A list of products that are on my shelf when it comes to my entire arsenal will be listed in chapter thirteen. In the long run, every medical mj farmer determines how the farm will be run.

DIPS

As a general practice, I use a dip when transplanting. A Dip can be compared to a spraying solution but in a less concentrated formula. A dip is not sprayed and usually only used on clones, seedlings, and small plants. Large plants are hard to dip and force you to spray. When using the dip, the entire plant makes contact with the dip solution, root ball and all.

My opinion is that *Azamax* is safe if not used thirty days prior to harvest. When transplanting from the plastic solo cup clone to the three- gallon pot, I prepare an *Azamax* dip in a five-gallon bucket. Wearing a good pair of clean rubber gloves, take your clone and seedlings in the plastic solo cups and remove the cup from the medium and roots (the root ball). Do this when the medium is somewhat dry instead of a freshly watered clone or seedling. The medium holds up in one piece better when it's a little dry. Being gentle, completely submerge the plant and the entire root ball. If you invert the clone plant, this allows the plant to get dipped first and the medium/root ball to get submerged last.

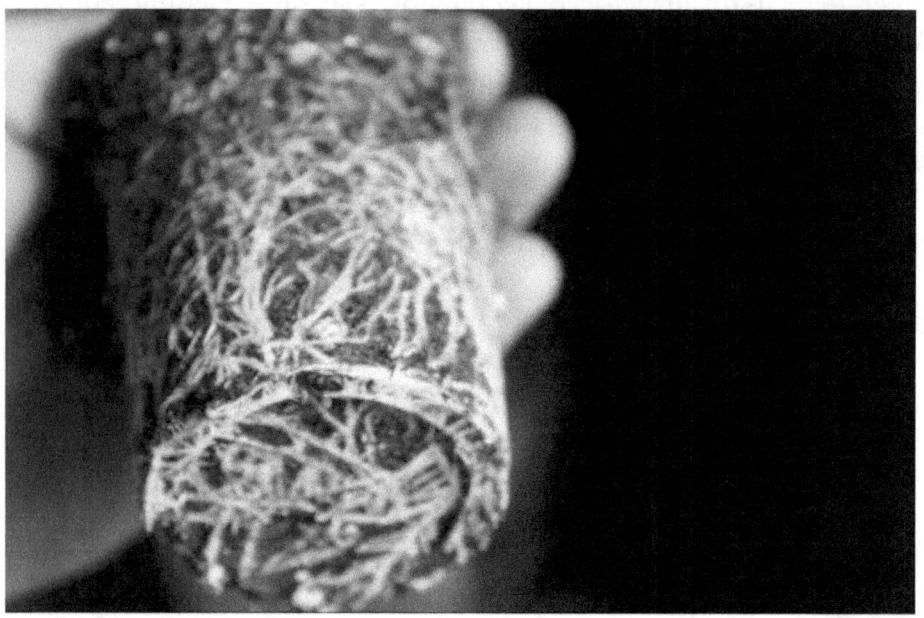

This is a root ball and almost ready for transplant.

This allows you to pull the root ball out first by holding the clone upside down while dipping. This allows the farmer to see how fast the medium is getting saturated. Only allow the medium to get fifty-percent saturated. Once the medium is more than fifty-percent wet, it can fall apart. This can rip roots that you have spent time and money growing.

Dipping at every transplant gives you peace of mind and potentially less work for a bug-free crop. Whenever my crop has spider mites, it stresses me out. I can have a crop of $60,000 - $100,000 net. It may not look like this much money when they are clones, but at outdoor harvest it sure will. When you reach for a product that's going to kill mites, you want it to work one hundred percent for the money and labor involved. When investing in a cash crop, you are growing a product that has more value than the USA dollar. Once you have acquired spider mites or powdery mildew, the farmer can try organic treatments. If results are not noticeable in two to three days, then screwing around with organic solutions would only turn out a weak and sick crop. This would result in less *net* income than previously mentioned. I recommend organic solutions as your first solution. But when in doubt, have all the products I recommend on the shelf in case you want to save your investment. I personally run a crop of ninety-percent clones and ten-percent seeds. If I dip, I try to do the entire crop. I dip whether the baby crop has bugs or not. By dipping you should technically be good for thirty days. If you want to try other methods at this stage, try homemade mixtures of lemon juice and hot pepper in place of *Azamax*. Half strength on dips is wise.

I am a firm believer of using all organic products and one-hundred-percent organic products thirty days prior to harvest. The problem with organic solutions is that you usually have to give them three to four days to see if they are working and additional days to see if they are completely, successful. My advice is: If running a big crop and you can see the organic solution is not successful within three to four days, then go with your alternative plan of solution for the problem. If I advise of an inorganic product or products in this book, it's because I went back to using an inorganic product after trying many organic products through trial and error. Always follow ethics and never apply anything poisonous to patients, thirty to sixty days prior to harvest. Always use your organic solution thirty days prior to harvest.

9

Germinating Seeds/ Sexing Seed Plants/ Hardening Off

If you are running seeds with clones on your home farm as I do, then make sure to mark everything. Keep the seedlings in one area and clones in another. My crop is ninety-nine in count and I do an inspection on every plant, every day, regardless of whether it is seed or clone.

When germinating seeds, start with shot glasses of treated water. If using different strains of medical mj, use a shot glass for each strain. Soak your seeds for twenty-for hours. Then prepare porcelain saucers for the seeds to germinate. Put a clean moist paper towel on the saucer. *Keyword: Moist,* not saturated. Fold the paper towel in to a size that fits on the saucer. Put your soaked seeds in between the layers of paper towel. Then cover and wrap the saucer with clear plastic food wrap. This keeps the paper towel from drying out. Do not wrap the plastic wrap too tightly. Allow for the breathability to be enough that you will have to moisten the paper towel every two days.

Check on the saucer every twelve to twenty-four hours to see if the paper towel needs more moisture/ treated water. Place your covered seed saucers on top of the refrigerator or in a kitchen cabinet high by the top of refrigerator. The small amount of heat that comes from behind a refrigerator rises up to the top. This allows for your ideal rooting temperature of seventy-eight to eighty-two degrees.

Your seeds probably cost you a decent amount of money. Prepare their home as well as you can so all of them pop roots. Never use cloning hormone on seeds. Seeds have their own natural hormones. Never use anything but treated water for seeds and seedlings until they are a foot tall or bigger. Seeds will germinate in two to seven days.

General rule of thumb is do not plan on using any germinated seeds after seven days. These could be weak seedlings and waste your time and money. Only plan on using the germinated seeds that pop a root in the first two to seven days. Using tweezers, gently place your germinated/rooted seed, root side down into your pre-wetted solo plastic cup. The seed should only be as deep as the total length of the germinated seed under the surface of the medium. Rock wool is *not* recommended for germinating seeds. Rock wool can retain a little too much moisture for germinated seeds. Rockwool is a risky home for seeds due to the chance of moldy seed, resulting in dead seed. Cocoa or cocoa pucks are satisfactory for germinating seeds. Your light for seedlings and rooted clones should be a continuous twenty-four hour fluorescent T5 light or eighteen hours light on and six hours off.

Word of advice: Do not grow seeds from someone who gives them to you. You could waste your time with unknown genetics. The person giving could be trying to waste your time. Buy seeds from a reputable seed bank.

I recommend through international mail: *Nirvana* seeds, and *Sensi* seeds. *Wait a minute!* There are reputable seed companies in Colorado. The TGA genetics *Subcool* seed company has a distributer in Denver. I recommend a seed they sell called Jilly Bean. For the beginner medical mj farmer, this strain grows noticeably on its own, with no nutrients. Once it is two to three feet high, you literally can kick it over, whether it's in a plant pot or not.... it will grow on its side. That's how strong it is. Jilly Bean has become such a favorite of some Coloradans that it is rumored that there is a Jilly Bean II. Jilly Bean has a good flavor, but what I like about it is its high, very mellow, like a hash high.

Seedlings should be checked on a daily basis as soon as they are six weeks old or less. I have seen seedlings start to show their sex (male or female) as early as six weeks. A quality magnifying glass is a valuable tool to have on the farm, not just for determining the sex of a medical mj plants but for close inspection for bugs and or determining a plant deficiency. An important rule of thumb is: Males usually show their sex first. Also, medical mj seedlings genetically will have the odds of producing fifty-percent males and fifty-percent females.

If you purchase feminized seeds, never assume that all the seeds are going to be female plants. Feminized seeds will only increase your odds of getting female plants and an inspection for sexing still needs to take place.

Auto-flowering seeds genetically do not need any special light to flower. They will automatically go into the flower cycle on their own. Auto-flowering strains of marijuana do not have the reputation of getting very big in plant size. They also have the reputation for not having very strong potency of THC.

You will make zero money from male seed plants in today's medical mj market. When sexing plants, hold the plastic solo cup in the light and your magnifying glass in the other. Pollen sacks look just like a pollen sack. A small round head on a small sprout-looking node. They will usually be located on the inner part of the branch at first indication. Female plants will sprout a small hair-looking node, known in grow terms as pre flower, reinforcing that males show their sex ninety- eight-percent sooner than the female will, but not always. Anticipate the removal of male plants from the farm in a large plastic trash bag. To ensure no pollen is on the farm, completely remove males from the property on a daily basis.

When clones and seedlings are in flower light (twelve-twelve) mode on indoor grows, they will show their sex almost immediately.

One way to sex seedling plants is by placing them in a flower room of twelve-twelve light and inspect everyday. Discard males, then put female seedlings back into vegetative mode of eighteen to twenty-four hour light and get them as big as you possibly can. A medical mj plant will still grow in size in the flower stage. I prefer to get them as big as possible in veg stage. On an outdoor grow this can be the inexpensive stage for getting the plant extra big. Bigger plant means bigger yield.

I prefer to sex my seedling medical mj plants under natural sunlight. This will be more gradual over time when it comes to the seedling showing its sex. Depending on what time of the year, the mj plants are taken outside. I generally try to take my medical mj plants outside on Mother's Day in order to save on electric costs. Which is minimal if only using fluorescent T5s. Watch the weather report for Mother's Day in Colorado. The *Farmers Almanac* is usually accurate. Some Colorado spring seasons are hot like summer, mid eighties to high eighties. Sometimes low nineties. Some spring seasons in Colorado can have snowstorms, every two weeks, and sometimes just after Mother's Day.

Hardening off is the process of getting your baby mj plants tough to the outdoor weather and natural sunlight. A small green house can be used to harden off the medical mj plants, or just leave them inside until after Mother's Day, depending on the weather forecast. If you are hardening off in sunlight without a greenhouse, placing the baby plants in a shaded area for a few days will allow them to adapt to natural sunlight easier. Depending on the strain of medical mj, if baby plants are taken in to direct sunlight they can wilt and lie down. They will stand back up under artificial light at night or help from a bamboo support. *Always*, try *not* to stress the plants. Good practices can save you work and maximize yield. I have been known to spoil my little babies and take them outside on nice days and bring them back in at night (small three gallon container/pot). They are literally like my children or pups. Most passionate medical mj farmers do take a true love for the work or it turns into just work. If the forecast for spring in Colorado is dry and hot, then use your H2O sprayer with treated water and cool mist early in morning and late at night. Mist a light spray only from above. Do not saturate. The light spray is just meant to keep the plant cells from being overly dry in a dry Colorado climate.

The weather in Colorado can run in a seven-year pattern. Although you may move to Colorado in the middle of a pattern, it is usually noticeable to have seven rainy springs then seven very hot and dry springs. Keeping this in mind along with a look at the *Farmer's Almanac* will help your outdoor planning.

Depending on the expected spring weather in Colorado, I use a black three-gallon pot when transplanting the plant from plastic solo cups. In order to keep lifting to a minimum, the three-gallon pots could be filled halfway. Choose your medium and prep these before the baby plants' roots appear when they will need a bigger growing medium. I prefer the three-gallon pot because I can still move the plants depending on anticipated weather. If the spring looks like it will be hot, then I will paint the outside of the black pot white.

This will help keep the roots from burning from a hot black pot. If it looks like it's going to be a cool spring, I will leave the black pots black. This may actually retain some heat that will help your roots grow. You cannot predict the weather, but you can follow patterns and the *Farmer's Almanac* is accurate. I will always paint my last and largest pot that I will be transplanting to white in color on the exterior. This is in effort to water less and keep roots from burning up along the sides of the pot. Your final pot size will depend on your budget. Every pot size holds a different amount of dirt. Pots are typically sold in a dark color to prevent light from getting through to the roots. Roots in nature are in the ground with complete darkness.

If your puppies are taking to the shade of a *powerplant*, then it is time to paint the pot/container white so the roots do not burn from heat of a black pot/container.

10

Raised Beds Are Less Work For The Beginner

If you are not growing ninety-nine medical mj plants, then you may want to consider raised beds. Raised beds are considerably less work, once the beds are prepared. A rototiller would be your best investment on this project and can be used year after year for preparation. Before constructing the raised beds, prep the existing ground with the rototiller. Then amend with your choice of fertilizers or soil conditioners. Cheap soil amendments are cocoa that keeps your dirt PH neutral, pea gravel helps the dirt retain water, chicken manure is a California medical-grower's secret (if you want to call that a secret) and great source of nitrogen for vegetative stage, bat guano for phosphorus, humus, cow manure, worm castings, and the soil conditioners go on as far as your wallet does, but the ones listed do just fine without anything else. Half-strength on soil conditioners is a good rule of thumb. Apply your soil conditioners on the surface of the rototilled ground, and pass over one more time with rototiller.

We can start construction of raised beds with four inch by four-inch lumber as your corner posts to fasten your two-inch by ten-inch plank lumber to. Now that the ground is soft you can get a four-inch by four-inch lumber post in the ground pretty easy with a hand sledgehammer. The raised-bed box can be one two by ten high or two courses high with two by ten. A battery-powered drill comes in handy. If you go two courses high with the two by tens, just use scrap pieces of two by four stud to fasten the two by tens together. Work the first course of two by ten into the medium before fastening to the four by four post at the corners. Since your dirt is soft, it will settle a little. You can foot pack at edges.

Once the raised bed is complete, your medium goes into the raised bed. Add additional four by four stakes, or two by four stakes to make things sturdy. Once the plants are three feet high, long lengths of two-inch by two-inch poles can be inserted into the ground and screwed to the two by tens. These poles will be used to hold a string lattice that will support your medical mj plants once the branches are heavy with buds. Periodically weave the plant branches through the lattice as the plant grows. The string lattice can be found at grow stores.

When constructing your raised beds, be certain to make them wide enough that the following spring you can just make a pass over the top of the raised beds with your rototiller. This keeps your work-load minimal year after year once your initial infrastructure is in place. Touch-up work may be a possibility, such as re-fastening your raised beds just to keep them tight and snug.

11

Organic versus Inorganic

Organic techniques should be your first option of defense. Your babies are easier to treat in an organic manner when they are small. Once they are the size of rhinos, they become difficult to manage organically. The biggest challenge is to get to harvest without powdery mildew and spider mites, these two problems being the more common in Colorado cultivation of marijuana. Both PM and spider mites occur easier in a dry climate *versus* a more humid climate. Although I have been known to get from the beginning to the end without using any inorganic compounds, the likelihood of having to use nonorganic products on a large outdoor grow is one to two applications per total run. Ultimately every farmer decides what to do with his/her investment.

I will try to stick to my list of rules. One of them is never bring people over to the farm until harvest, and even then it should be selective choices of trim personal. In Colorado, your helpers and friends will most likely be working for other medical mj farmers and dispensaries. This is how big the industry is, and an example of one host that can contaminate your crop from being at other farms that are potentially contaminated with something you do not want at your place of medicine.

Taking a shower and having clean clothes is a good practice before entering the farm or grow room.

The practice of ladybugs to eat spider mites can be effective in a greenhouse or grow room. Mark the plant or plants that are spider mite infested. Have your bug nets/bug bags available along with your lady- bugs. If your local grow store does not have ladybugs, I recommend the Internet. Overnight shipping is the normal procedure. There is a variety of bugs that are available to purchase that are even more specific to eating spider mites than the ladybug. One theory is: *If* the bug on the plant is not causing problems (example: eating holes in leaves) then it can be left alone, because it could be eating harmful bugs (another example: Praying Mantis).

The bug netting that will cover the entire plant like a large trash bag, including the pot, can sometimes be found at garden centers in the form of frost-protective bags. These would only be suitable for small plants typically. I recommend a camping supply catalog. They will have a sleeping-bag-size, bug netting. These tools should all be in stock before your potential spider-mite problems occur. You will only have two to three days before the plant is infested and maximum yield will not be reachable.

A word to the beginner is neem oil does not work as a cure for spider mites. You can spend all the money you want on neem oil as a preventative, but it's not recommended as a preventative in Colorado. In general, Colorado is too dry of a climate for neem oil to be effective.

Leaf Miners are fairly harmless. But if they look like they are spreading, just remove the leaves that they are living in.

Keep in mind bugs can bring other bugs into a grow room or farm. They can piggyback on flies and fly legs. So keeping bugs to a minimum is good idea. If harmless bugs seem to be in large numbers and you need to control them, try organic sticky traps. They can be wired to the base of the plant in the lower branches. They can also be placed on the floor or ground or up high tied to an oscillating fan stand.

Powdery mildew can be treated effectively and organically with potassium bicarbonate, not to be confused with any other variations

Pictured is a red ribbon marking a plant with Leaf Miners. Marking plants makes them very easily identifiable if there is a specific problem. Also note the organization of plants by the kind of marijuana strain.

of potassium make ups, what so ever. Outdoor farmers will have to re-apply this if and when they encounter rainfall. Potassium bicarbonate is only effective for thirty days before it needs to be re-applied without rainfall. I recommend first use of potassium bicarbonate at half-strength of directions on container. Try it as a preventative, at half-strength. Different strains can be sensitive to sprays. Be cautious, especially if used as a preventative and there is no sign of PM. All spraying, outdoor and indoor, should be done in low light, just after sunrise and just before sunset. Spraying and direct light do not work in any situation. Burning could occur and stress would result, effecting maximum yield. If PM is obviously present on the farm, the best practice of using potassium bicarbonate spray is to drench the plant as if soaking the top of leaves and under side of leaves. Potassium bicarbonate is the safest organic remedy to powdery mildew problems and has no harm to the consumer/ patient whatsoever. The drawback is the money and labor involved on outdoor farms, if it rains.

Although sulfur can be effective against bugs (spider mites), and powdery mildew it is not recommended as a spray. In Colorado and across the USA, the medical mj user has acquired such a coneisour-taste for medical mj that just the slightest bit of sulfur can be smelled and tasted. Sulfur can be effective but your crop could be compromised on the odor and flavor of the medical mj at harvest. If sulfur is an only option, start with the weakest sulfur solution possible. If it does not show noticeable signs that it is working within two to three days, then increase the concentration of the sulfur mix. Chances are that if the sulfur is a noticeable sulfur odor when spraying then it will most likely be noticeable at bud-curing time and even possibly at edible time. This sulfur odor should not be a problem if a sulfur burner is used on an indoor grow or greenhouse. Sulfur burners are effective for indoor use and recommended.

If these solutions to spider mites and powdery mildew do not work for the beginner, I list other products I use in a later chapter that not only have been proven worthy to have on the shelf, but some of which originated in California. Some came from trial and error, which the author used after trying many, many products.

Although starting a crop from seed, or even a portion of it from seed, allows for first-generation clones for the next run, it also allows you to have clean plants that have no problems with bugs or mold. Key is keeping your practice good and your farm and grow room clean. When running a large crop, have these products on the shelf. You may need to *save* your investment just as I have had to do a couple of times.

When using liquid nutrients, a watered-down nitrogen, phosphate, and potassium would be valuable when giving your babies their first nutrients at twelve inches to eighteen inches high. When medical mj starts to get big in the vegetative stage, it can use higher levels of nitrogen. During 'flower stage' you will want phosphates and potassium and a lower level of nitrogen. These are general guidelines. I would like to inform you of specific products I have had success with when it comes to liquid nutrients.

If wanting to stay organic, then I suggest the *Botanicare* line as your best for your U.S. dollar. If you are not concerned about staying organic, then I will suggest *FoxFarm*. *Big Bloom* is the only liquid fertilizer that I am aware that *FoxFarm* carries that is considered organic in their basic line. It is my belief that *FoxFarm*-basic line will give you the biggest yield and incredible aroma and density.

Non-organic fertilizers can be very effective, and have a bad rap. They *can* be flushed from the medium prior to harvest. *FoxFarm*-basic line can and will give you the most bang for your buck.

There are ethics when using pesticides and systemic mold sprays when you are close to harvest. These ethics will be discussed with the specific products in chapter thirteen.

12

General Business Guidelines

Medical mj dispensaries are required by Colorado State regulations to have security cameras at all entrances and exits and throughout the entire business, including the dispensary, the grow facility, and any commercial kitchen that may be making bi-products. The dispensary camera system can be compared to the gaming/ casino industry. An inventory book of medical mj transported is kept, because dispensaries are allowed to buy and sell medical mj to other dispensaries. There is also a medical mj plant tagging system to keep track of every plant for size, yield, or even death for whatever reason.

These are all things that can be learned when it comes to the residential caregiver grow/farm. In actuality, the dispensary is a caregiver or partnership of caregivers. The plant-tagging system was started by caregivers in residential grows. It carried over to the dispensary owners (caregivers). The state of Colorado adopted the tagging system in the dispensary regulations. Caregivers have been tagging mj plants in Colorado for well over ten years.

As a caregiver operating as a residential grow or farm, keep some type of book even if you don't file a tax return reporting caregiving and medical mj. The reason you would not file a tax return is because you are a beginner just trying to grow six plants to see if the business is for your stomach or not.

If you are growing a sizable crop and trying to make an income, I *suggest* keeping receipts of your costs, the square footage use in the home for the business, and water, electric utilities, and any considerable mileage involved. These records are not only good for preparing a tax return, but also for your journal and general farming records. 1) How much you invested (capital upfront). 2) How much you spent for medium and pots. 3) Pot size. 4) Bamboo supports, mortgage, or rent payment, bud-trimming costs, plastic bags for packaging, etc. All information you can look at for the next crop.

For example, you are considering doubling your plants, pot (container) size, and plant numbers. Last year's records will give an idea how much the extra dirt will cost and the pot container costs. Of course you are subtracting your costs from your gross income to find the net.

The tagging of plants was first started by residential caregiver growers/farmers. If the caregiver was growing a sizable crop, he would put the name of the patients he or she was growing the medical mj for on the tag or write the name of the patient on the pot. This practice has slowly gone away and the paperwork for up-to-date extended plant counts are what is relied upon foremost. The dispensary acquired the system for reasons of claiming on a tax report/return that fifty plants died. It can happen. Rare, but it can happen. The State of Colorado liked the tagging system of the dispensaries and has made it part of the State regulations for tracking the plant from beginning to end. The tagging system is now part of the camera system. The State of Colorado is allowed to view the camera information that is recorded for twenty-four hours' round the clock.

I recommend if any caregivers have credit from suppliers in any other businesses to try to set up wholesale accounts for your growing supplies. Ask the grow supplier if you can use a supplier you have used for ten years in another business as a referral. It will save you capital in the long run, leading to more net profit. Another solution to wholesale pricing is to offer a credit card payment if you can set up a wholesale account or at least discounted pricing.

Marijuana is profitable, but as a farmer getting it from beginning to end is a costly process. I spend more on bud trimming than I care to even think about. Also, drying, curing and bagging, and storing. My advice: To be good in this business, save the net income from the first few pounds that you sell, and put that cash toward bud-trimming costs. The next five to ten pounds sold should be saved for your costs for the next farming run. Once you ensure you still have a job by having some business costs taken care of, then you can count a little profit. Do not forget your costs for the next year in rent or mortgage payments. Go ahead, have a cheeseburger. I do not recommend buying a Porsche.

The biggest advice I can give is to never have anyone living with you or helping on your medical mj farm. They would only steal from you sooner than later. Only farm as much as you can by yourself. You can and will save yourself some peace of mind. You will need to have trimmers help you at harvest. The trimmers at medical marijuana dispensaries have a criminal background check required by the state of Colorado. I recommend the dispensary trimmers and ask for their dispensary employee *badge* ID so you can take a photo of it with your cell phone to have on file. Do not let your gaze off them. Just currently having a clean criminal record does not mean they won't have a bad one in the future. These types of trimmers can be found at popular eateries or bars in the dispensary neighborhoods. Just ask the waitresses or bartenders. They know these trimmers by their aromas. I have also been known to use trimmers to help with work other than trimming.

In Colorado, some accountants are biased and will not prepare your tax return just because you're a marijuana farmer. If you decide to prepare a return, determine if you're in it for a hobby or income. You should have no problems finding an accountant in Colorado. You may decide to do the return yourself, as most Americans do.

I had established two small businesses that did well during an okay economy. The economy took a turn for the worse due to the USA government and the banking industry, turning many Coloradans to turn to medical mj farming. They say that history repeats itself.

Could this have been what happened during the Great Depression and hemp farmers? (It is opinion and advice to anyone successful in the medical mj industry to create depth in your personal portfolio.)

Real estate is starting to show signs of coming back in the Denver area and suburbs. This is partly due to the fact that there is a very low inventory of homes for sale because the inventory in foreclosure is enormous. The smart thing to do is to put some profits into real estate that can produce more medical mj. Even if you can not physically grow more medical mj than you already are, the resale value on homes set up for at- home business of medical mj has a market value of sixty-percent higher than average. The set up could be home improvements as little as clean rooms, beefing up the electrical work with an electrician, and having a good location. You are now in what is called a sellers' market.

Colorado has the strongest regulations on marijuana in the world. At the dispensary level of business, marijuana is over regulated and over taxed because of the over regulations. Court cases will be brought against the over regulations over time. The cases can be on the basis of how alcohol and other goods are taxed.

Although this book is about medical mj, I have seen successful medical mj dispensary owners open eateries next to the dispensary. Once the dispensary customers know the dispensary owner owns the eatery next door, it creates a domino effect in transactions. Yes, Colorado's economy is coming back thanks to medical mj and recreational pot. Very trendy areas of Denver have large numbers of restaurants. Washington Park and Highlands are just a couple.

People have put a number on the percentage that medical mj has stimulated the Colorado state economy, but any number calculated would only be speculation. Better individual state economies improve the national economy, even if the majority of the states are in bad shape.

13

Favorite Growing Products that make it a pleasure and rewarding

Well, after chapter 12, I hope you still want to grow marijuana. This is the chapter that I hope gets used. So many grow products are available that it could take you a decade just to try the ones that you want. That is, if you have the money to buy them. But these are the ones that are the best for your dollar.

Cocoa is a medium mentioned in this book. Cocoa bricks are your best value if you have the time to do a little work. If you have the time to do a lot of work, then I suggest a small, cheap cement mixer for your medium mix. I use a cement mixer just for the cocoa, peat, and pea-gravel portion of the medium. All the fertilizer/ soil conditioners are added by hand. Get the help of the strong back of a house boy/ helper, who needs extra work/ income. If you have the money to spend on labor for pots and dirt preparation, spend it. I always feel like I am doing my civil duty by giving people jobs.

If you can't find a reasonable price on large pots, then brown plastic trashcans can be used. When selecting a pot/container always use a dark plastic color, such as black or dark brown. You absolutely do not want light getting through the plastic to the roots. Roots do not like light. Always make drain holes if they do not already exist.

This cocoa brick is used as fifty percent of the
medium blend to be used in the author's pots/containers.

Sunshine Mix is a big peat/perlite blend that is very popular in Colorado. All peat mixes work. Try to stick to a Canadian peat. Although not considered a one-hundred-percent peat product, *FoxFarm's Ocean Forest Blend* has much more than just peat. This is a mix that is just about fail proof and can be used in your pot, standing alone by itself without adding anything else from beginning to end but just treated water. It is a little pricey, but takes the brainwork out of pot/medium ingredients and making your own mix, and labor. *FoxFarm* also sells potting soils that are partially peat that are not as good as the *Ocean Forest Blend* but are great for the price.

Pea-gravel can be purchased from aggregate suppliers by the ton for absolutely no more than thirty dollars per ton, or less. You will need a pick-up/ farm truck for this transport. You can use clean five gallon buckets in another vehicle if you do not have a truck. Pea-gravel substitutes for the very expensive *Hydroton* and can be substituted for the expensive perlite, also.

Since I am a fan of *FoxFarm*, an organic solution can be achieved with *FoxFarm* products by using the *FoxFarm* soil fertilizers/ conditioners such as *JumpStart* and bat guano. Or stand alone *FoxFarm Oceanforest* Blend. In order to remain organic, use only treated water from beginning to end.

Although the *FoxFarm* basic liquid fertilizer line is not considered organic, it is very water-soluble and flushes easily from the medium.

Light will be discussed in the next chapter, but inducers will be listed in this chapter. Inducers or early-flowering products are products of high phosphorus content and used when the sign of pre-flower is obvious. The most inexpensive one is *FoxFarm's OpenSesame*. The more expensive product is made by a company called *MOAB*. Which stands for *Mother of All Bloom*. Using nutrients in the treated water to feed plants should always be used at half-strength. The reason is because the medical mj plants may and probably could be being fed more than once per day. This adds up to full strength in the course of a twenty-four hour period or stronger if fed more than twice a day. An outdoor farming example is the month of August when the

This is obvious pre-flower.

heat requires not only a morning feed but evening water also. Half-strength in morning and half-strength at night equals full strength. Consider just straight treated water for the evening feed. This saves on costs and the morning feed before 10:00am is the crucial time for outdoor plants to have their nutrient feed.

FoxFarm's Open Sesame does not work on all strains of medical mj, but it will be effective on eighty-five to ninety-five percent of strains. It can and will save the farmer two to four weeks time on the flower stage. When pre-flower is obvious, it should be used to advance the first week of bud development and growth. You will see the female plant go from pre flower to not a penny-or-nickel size bud, but in five to seven days the size of a quarter. With outdoor Colorado crops, the sooner a crop goes through its flower stage the better. Not every Halloween gets snow and cold, but just in case, *Open Sesame.* You are saving time and money to get product to the scale by using the high phosphorus *Open Sesame.* Buds can sometimes take a month to achieve the quarter size without the *Open Sesame.*

The use of *MOAB* is a considerable cost and only recommended for use if medical mj strains do not respond to *Open Sesame.*

Molasses is a source of nitrogen. Not incredibly high in nitrogen content, but some. During the vegetative stage and flower stage of medical mj plant growth, natural plant sugars develop, more in the flower-stage. Molasses can be used in vegetative stage as a mild nitrogen source, but it helps the natural plant sugars develop and gives the plant more natural odor, even with tomatoes. The use of molasses will also give fruit/flowers a sweeter flavor. In the vegetative stage, use molasses at half-strength. In the flower stage, the dose can be used at regular strength, especially during the flushing period before harvest. The best part of molasses is that it is organic and inexpensive and can give medical mj a sweeter taste and five-percent more density to buds at the scale. Molasses will help with crystal/ trichome development during flower stage. Do not over due it with molasses. Too much can kill the plant.

Romulan is a good one. It gets very dense and has a citrus odor.

Emerald Triangle or *Humboldt Counties Own* sell a product called *Gravity* or G-10. This product can make your medical mj buds very dense. It will be noticeable at the scale. It works more consistently with medical mj strains that are genetically dense. I would not recommend trying to use *Gravity* on medical mj strains that are genetically fluffy. If you like your buds to hit the scale like glass marbles, then try it. If you can't find it, then contact me. *General Hydroponics* has had a product out for a couple years that is very similar to *Gravity*. As recommended throughout this book, use all liquid nutrients being added to the feeding water at half strength, this means *Gravity* also. One other product I recommend by *Emerald Triangle* is *Crystal Burst*. It can and does help with crystal/ trichome development.

Cal/Mag is a product I recommend having on the shelf. It is a calcium/magnesium supplement. I recommend *Botanicare* brand *Cal/Mag* because it is organic and you will not find a name brand for much cheaper, if at all. *Cal/Mag* is used at half-strength if the medical mj plants have yellow or brown spots that appear to potentially be a threat to the health of the leaves. If leaves are unhealthy, this means less maximum yield. Leaves should be dark green in color at all times. If the plant seems not so dark green, then experiment with *Cal/Mag* for the look you want, in order to achieve maximum yield. *Cal/Mag* at half dose is harmless to the plant. If yellow or brown spots on leaves do exist, check with your magnify glass on the under side of leaves for spider mites, bug eggs, or other bugs. Yellow, white, and brown spots can also be sign of white flies. Regardless, a farmer has to be prepared to solve problems if they arrive. Solve your spotted-leaf problem systematically. Check for bugs first. If no signs of bugs then use half strength *Cal/Mag* supplement in your feed.

Azamax is one of the most common miticides used in Colorado. The spider mite can build resistance to miticides and should be treated by a different miticide on consecutive plant treatment. If a medical mj plant is treated with the same miticide time after time, the spider mite can become resistant. For outdoor use, *Azamax* has taken a backseat to *Avid insecticide* only because *Azamax* can wash off the plant during rainy weather and *Avid* can't. *Azamax* is still a great and effective miticide. Both products *should not* be used thirty days prior to harvest or you will be smoking these products mentioned. Here is where the ethics are involved. I personally do not know anyone who has used these products unethically. These two products are considered safe to use up until thirty days prior to harvest. Some farmers will stop use sixty to ninety days prior to harvest to guarantee the plant is free of the product. This product is only advised for use if your organic solution to the problem is not successful. Colorado medical mj farmers growing large crops will use one of these products or both. If they are not using them, then the large farmers have these two products on the shelf for potential use. Alternate the use of the two mentioned products every needed application. Spider mites can and do build resistance to one individual product.

Eagle 20 is a fail proof product that first started being used by the grape industry in California. It is widely used for powdery mildew. Once sprayed on the plant, it cannot wash off from rainstorms. It goes in to the cells of the plant and does not need to be applied again for another thirty days. It cannot be used thirty days prior to harvest or you will be smoking the chemical. Some farmers will stop use sixty to ninety days prior to harvest to guarantee the plant is free of the product. This product is only recommended as a solution to PM if at first your organic solution of potassium bicarbonate does not work. Potassium bicarbonate should always work but the outdoor farmer may get frustrated with PM if it's raining on a daily basis. Powdery mildew can greatly affect the maximum yield. Powdery mildew will eat crystals and buds. If powdery mildew is not controlled, it will affect your net worth. Sulfur was mentioned earlier as a spray not recommended for PM. Although sulfur sprays are not recommended, sulfur burners are very effective against bugs and powdery mildew. The problem with sulfur burners is they are only effective indoors or in greenhouses.

Hi-Yield makes the most in-expensive bug bomb. Also referred to in the state of Colorado as a grenade. These are commonly used in indoor grow rooms or greenhouses. Very effective against the spider mite and should be part of the marijuana farmer's arsenal, if starting babies indoors. The bomb or grenade saves on time and labor. Be sure not to put it too close to plants. You are trying to bomb the entire room, not one plant. Once again, this product is not intended for use thirty days prior to harvest.

The following three *FoxFarm* products are recommended as stock to have in inventory.

FoxFarm does sell organic products. The entire line of products together, are not known as an organic name-brand. *FoxFarm* sells much more than just the following products but I have had my best run using less than more. *FoxFarm's Grow Big* is a nitrogen product for the vegetative stage. It is not organic but works incredibly well and is easily flushed from soil/ dirt/ medium. I would concentrate on medical mj strains that need nothing but treated water. Having *FoxFarm's GrowBig* on the shelf allows for a quick correction of nitrogen deficiency. The best rule of thumb is: If the plant is yellowing or just not a dark lush green, then ask yourself 1) could I be over watering? Yellowing or leaves that are not a dark lush green could be getting too much water. 2) Inspect with your hand-held magnifying glass for spider mites, especially under the leaves. Spider mites and other bugs and bug eggs living under leaves are a common problem of yellowing leaves. If there is no sign of spider mites then 3) try a half-strength mix of *FoxFarm's Grow Big*. Yellowing or the lack of dark green color in leaves can be a nitrogen deficiency. If your medical mj plants are nitrogen deficient then they will get lush dark green again two to four days.

FoxFarm Big Bloom is primarily known for its flowering qualities, but it can be used at half-strength or less for small medical mj plants at twelve inch high. The phosphate and potassium can be useful to small plants.

FoxFarm Tiger Bloom and *FoxFarm BigBloom* have been known for their flowering qualities in California for decades. A half-strength solution every other day should work. If you see an incredible difference from these products, then try half strength everyday.

Water filtration for medical mj plants has always been a cost to the indoor farmer. Outdoor *medical mj* farming is easier and treated water is inexpensive. A chlorine/heavy-metal neutralizer can be found at a pet store in the fish tank department for the treatment of fish tank water.

Specific products mentioned in this chapter can be purchased for the purpose of making medical mj buds dense. This chapter is specifically intended to help your investment reach the scale in the best possible bud form. If you are going to do the work, then you might as well have the heaviest, odoriferous, and stickiest crop that you can.

Although cane sugar is not recommended on the shelf, it can be stored somewhere that will guarantee that it will not attract bugs. If cane sugar is added to a medical mj plant it will kill the plant. Technically if you cut the plant down at harvest, you are killing the plant.

This technique can be used at harvest when cutting down your plants. Sugar can add ten-to-fifteen percent more density to medical mj buds. This is how to use sugar to give added weight at the scale. When any species of plant or plant branch is cut and placed in a glass of water, the plant will uptake the water. Do your own experiment. Cut a branch of any plant and stick it in a glass of water. It can and will live sometimes well past two weeks.

Prepare five to six clean five gallon buckets. Fill the buckets eighty-five to ninety percent full of water. Add the sugar to the water. These sugar water buckets can be prepared two to three days before harvest to ensure that your sugar is good and dissolved in the water. Place the five-gallon bucket of sugar water in a corner of a cool room. Cut one of your medical mj plants down for harvest having clear or slightly amber-colored crystals/ trichomes. Make sure you leave a long

Lemon Poison is a tasty medicine.

trunk/ stem so it will stick in to the sugar water. The lower branches of the plant will keep the plant from being submerged in sugar water. It's the same concept as keeping a Christmas tree alive for a couple weeks. The medical mj plant leaves will turn yellow, if they have not during flower stage already from phosphorus. The plant will not stay alive because there is sugar in the water. Only leave the MMJ plant in the sugar water a maximum of one to two days. It will most likely start to have a dead and wilted look to it. What we do not want is the plant to have a smell like it's starting to rot. We do not want to affect the natural odor of the plant that we worked so hard to achieve. If in doubt, less time soaking than longer.

Hang the medical mj plant upside down and let it dry in your drying room. Nice slow dry time of two weeks in a cool, dark room. Using fans and ventilation. Repeat, cool and dark. If a large amount of plants are in a room, do not hesitate to use a dehumidifier. Once you reach a goal of one point five pounds per plant then I suggest to keep using your recipe. It's all about preparation, good repetition, and repeat recipes that worked for you in the past.

I try to learn something from everyone I run in to. I have learned lots from kids, mostly tech stuff like cell phones. It is funny to watch kids switch to *FoxFarm* once they see the size of the medical marijuana plants and the healthy dark green lush color it provides. One of the main reasons *FoxFarm* should be used is because of its price. It is considerably cheaper than most everything on the shelf. Try it before you decide on something expensive.

For the outdoor farmer, use the products suggested for nutrient feeding in the morning hours of daylight. The medical mj plants prefer to be fed in the morning and will use the money you are giving them more productively during the day than at dusk. Preferably before ten AM. The same applies to indoor farmers. Set your timers on your drip systems/flood table for feeding just after the lights come on. Grow rooms usually set the timers to feed more than once a day. But the feed that happens just after the lights come on is the most valuable feed to note.

14

Light - Natural And Artificial

This book primarily focuses on outdoor growing of medical mj because it will give you the best return on your investment. Outdoor light is superior to indoor. With outdoor light, it is important not to have any shade and get the most direct sunlight available. This is what is trying to be achieved in an indoor situation.

When preparing an outdoor medical mj farm or even leasing or buying a property, look for southern exposure first and foremost. Southern exposure means that your crop faces south and has no obstructions from the southern side of the property line. For example, an obstruction would be a building or large amounts of trees. With southern exposure, a farm will get sunlight as soon as the sun rises until the time that it sets in the west. Shade needs to be avoided. Cut down trees or bushes or trim in order to achieve maximum light and yield.

Light is better than any nutrient. You can make your grow room brighter than the actual sun itself, if you want. The indoor farmer always has to deal with the problems of heat from grow lights through ventilation. Vertical lighting on walls has not been proven to be a substantial benefit. White-painted walls or reflective poly plastic has better benefit than vertical lighting. The general rule for indoor farmers is five to six medical mj plants per light. If you want to overdue it with lighting from the ceiling this is okay, just consider the added ventilation. Medical mj plants will respond to good light more than nutrients. Additional light can be prepared on outdoor farms. Painting a garage or property fence white helps reflect light. The use of reflective poly plastic can also be fastened in areas or corner that may be a little shaded.

This reflective material is used with indoor grow rooms.
It is also helping an outdoor farm.

It is not recommended to put reflective material or mirrors on the floor or ground surfaces, on either indoor or outdoor farms. Plants are not used to receiving light from the underside of the leave.

Outdoor medical mj farmers have to be aware of additional light coming from neighboring properties at nighttime. The metal halide of a streetlight or the flood light of a neighbor's garage may be enough to seed a female medical mj crop. This amount of light encroaching at night will only cause two to five seeds per plant. This amount of seeds could easily be removed at bud trimming time.

In any case, the outdoor farmer should do everything possible to keep the outdoor crop from being exposed to light. If the farmhouse is adjacent to the medical mj farm, then cover the windows with a black covering to keep extra light from getting through to the farm plants. Black plastic can work if used on the indoor side of the window. Indoor growing rooms are very common in Colorado and growing lights should absolutely not be visible from outside the home at nighttime. It makes big security problems because people can tell you are growing indoors if they see the grow light. Grow light is very distinctive and bright. A lot of people in Colorado know what it looks like.

Full moons can even seed a crop. Shade cloth at nighttime on a green house is a considerable cost, but the results will be a faster flowering process from beginning to end, with no seeds.

A Flood light on a garage very close to the medical mj farm is a definite threat during flower stage on the outdoor crop. The simple removal of bulbs from fixtures during the flower stage would be insurance that no one is flicking a light switch on by mistake.

Green light is used during the flower stage of indoor and outdoor farming to check on flowering crops during the dark/ nighttime periods. It is not recommended on a motion sensor where a crop could be exposed to this green light on a daily/ nightly basis. Although it would not completely hermaphrodite a female plant, it could potentially give you twelve to twenty seeds per plant. The main idea is to keep your nighttime light to a very minimum.

If in doubt and running a big investment, purchase a light meter that measures lumens at nighttime. The cheap light meters do not work, so do not waste your money.

Indoor medical mj farmers will experience seeding or hermaphrodite plants depending on how much light is getting into the flower room on the lights-out cycle. It's very important to test your flower room. Just sit in there with the lights off and look for the slightest bit of light getting into the flower room. Sit in the flower room for five minutes, letting your eyes adjust to the darkness. Doorways and windows are the obvious areas but around vents and walls are not so obvious. Old homes or poorly built ones can let light through walls. The flower room is to be completely dark when lights are off. Foam in a spray can is good for hard-to-get cracks where light is getting through.

Notes to remember for outdoor farmers are dates that will help you if it looks like a possible spring snow, you may want to plan on keeping babies inside until two weeks after Mother's Day. A small green house can be used to put a large amount of small plants. Leave the greenhouse up the entire run, and just have four to six large ones in there at flower stage. If a greenhouse is used, allow for a space heater. Large spring snowstorms in Denver can cause a temperature dip. Watch the weather report. Cold temperatures as low as thirty-three degrees can stop plant growth. The babies should be kept cozy for maximum yield.

The small greenhouse in a cool spring can be a good idea for the strongest of the crop. Hardening off in a greenhouse would be good preparation for healthy medical mj plants that may be bracing for up-and- down spring weather. Remember, they are babies.

So when you prepare for a cold night with a heater, experiment on low setting during the day. Check your thermometer and make the proper heater setting for night temps. Don't cook the babies. A greenhouse is not considered direct sunlight, so greenhouse light is good for hardening off. Greenhouses can be good for CO_2 experimentation, which can give extra crystals and bud density. CO_2 should be applied in a foliar feed application from above with a fan. Depending on the size of the greenhouse, you could have the problem of the plants getting to tall and taking them outside, anyway.

Taking one-foot high plants outside on Mother's Day can cause the plant to pre flower. It does not always happen, but the plants have been in artificial light on a pattern of eighteen to twenty-four hour lights *on*. Taking them outside to harden off on Mother's Day or close to that date, puts the plants in a light pattern slightly shorter than the eighteen hour pattern. Don't worry, the plant will revert back to the vegetative stage. It depends on the strain of medical mj and the intensity of the spring sunshine. Hot spring seasons usually do not cause pre flower. By going in to pre flower, the plant is switching hormones. To revert one time is okay, but reverting back and forth, veg to flower, flower to veg, over and over can weird the plant out. This causes plant hormone confusion, which effects maximum yield.

It's my experience that premature pre-flowering consistently occurs less often when hardening off in a greenhouse.

Two-day spring snowstorms may have you bringing small containers of plants back inside or in a prepared greenhouse. Hardening off is usually a gradual period of a week to ten days where plants will be outdoors for one to three hours. This depends on the many spring weather factors of direct sunlight versus clouds, temperature, high-winds, etc. The day to take plants outdoors fulltime is anytime between Mother's Day and Summer Solstice. Summer Solstice usually falls on June 20th or 21rst. The start of transplanting the first crop to your biggest and final container can start anywhere between Mother's Day and Summer Solstice. Check your root balls. If there are plenty-of-roots, consider transplanting. Too many roots jammed in a small container can cause *root lock*. Do your weather research before transplanting because moving a heavy large container can hurt a back. Timing is key and you should have a feel for all your plants at this point on.

Labor Day is when medical mj plants should be at their biggest possible size, in the veg stage. Medical mj plants will continue to grow in size in the flower stage. The purpose of getting plants as big as possible during the veg stage not only means height but also thickness of branches to hold heavy buds and thick trunks to hold up to wind and weather. Try to get your vegetative plants like trees to hold your apples.

The medical mj plants can start to pre flower just after Labor Day. These shorter days of sunlight are when they should be inspected closely by the farmer. Once a half dozen to a dozen of a specific strain show pre flower, then *FoxFarm Open Sesame* can be used once a week at half strength. The entire crop can be induced to flower or you can induce by strain. This is where having your crop marked by strain allows you to manage it better and only spend the money on *Open Sesame* as needed, when the *time* comes.

Halloween in Colorado can sometimes be the first good cold snap. Outdoor farmers should watch the weather report for two weeks prior to and following Halloween. Temperatures can reach overnight lows of twenty degrees F or less, depending on the year. A warm spring snow can be harmless, but fall snow is unpredictable and usually means frost. This could be damaging to trichome/ crystals that have been developing for two months or less. This is where *FoxFarm Open Sesame* helps the outdoor farmer keep his crop developed and finished before snow moves in, saving the need to try to reach full bud maturity in a snowstorm or frost–which would most likely end the lifecycle of most of the medical mj plants.

15

Keeping a journal

This can be easy in today's world. Notes can be taken in a cell phone and emailed to a computer for organization at a later period. Date your notes and put a subject or topic line for easier management later.

Taking notes on your crop is important. You will only take photos or limited notes on another farmer's medical mj crop. Specifics are from beginning to end. You may use different strains every crop, but much better decision is to grow the strains you have had success with in prior crops as the bulk of a new crop. Only try new strains to a limited degree until you see how they perform and their final outcome. The truth is, three clones off the same mother can be given to three different farmers, and they could all get different results. The medical mj business is similar to other trades in the sense that you pick mentors. The real teachers in today's world will only teach if they have the time and if you seem to be a student who can be trained. It takes special motivational skills to teach and the ones who have knowledge do not necessarily know how to teach.

In Colorado, a lot of medical mj strains exist to choose from. Real medical mj farmers have the experience of growing different strains. The strains that will stand out in their memories will be the kinds that made them a lot of money (yield), potency, aroma, and crystals. You will probably be one of very few keeping a journal. The numbers do not lie, and a journal can refresh your memory as to the best ones.

Start your journal from the very beginning. You may choose to use a different rooting hormone every crop. You may get your seeds from a different seed bank for this crop. What strains you run every crop is important. The consistency of the health of the seeds you received. What date you started and finished crops. Weather. What line of nutrients you choose to use year after year. What kind of dirt/medium did you use this year? What size pot was used? Which strains achieved enormous tree- like size during the vegetative period? All may have been factors for a better yield that year.

Which strains of medical mj were sensitive to cool misting at the larger size of three feet tall? These would be the strains that prefer to be fed religiously from the dirt and roots. Having a medical mj plant that is sensitive to a cool mist just saves the farmer work. Record in your journal the specific recipe you used for the dirt mix and the recipe for the nutrient feed. How much time did you spray products for Powdery Mildew and the cost of the spray? Is there a certain bug that organically took care of spider mites better than another? The journal is one of the best tools a person can use, not only for farming but, for fly-fishing. If you do not care to use an android device, use a note pad and pen. Memory is not the best thing to rely on for specifics seven to ten years later.

A journal and your receipts and billing invoices will help you manage your costs year to year and help you keep it simple to grow big crops of medical mj. Stick with the repetitions that work for you.

16

The Checklist

W rite the checklist on a piece of paper and post it in the grow room or very nearby an outdoor farm along with a calendar. Check the checklist frequently and refer to it often. The checklist can also be put in a notes section of a cell phone. Plan the days of your week based on the chores on the checklist. All of the things listed on the checklist do not need to be done every day. But all of the chores listed should be done once per week. When choosing a day of the week for one of the chores on the list, also include an inspection for spider mites and powdery mildew on a daily basis. The checklist develops good habits and repetition in an individual farmer and over years, instinct.

This is a checklist all medical marijuana farmers should follow.

When preparing a grow room for clones, vegetative plants, or flowering plants, a common practice is to bomb the room for spider mites first. This is where your aerosol bug bomb (grenade) comes in to play.

A spray bottle, or depending on the size of grow, a sprayer specifically for a bleach solution. Take a black magic marker and mark it *bleach* so nothing else gets mixed in this sprayer but bleach. Bleach solution of ten-percent bleach to ninety-percent water is the mix needed. Never spray bleach directly on medical mj plants or in the medium. It can be used on surfaces when cleaning. Once a month or more often, bleach can be sprayed on the floor around plants. Make sure not to get it in saucers if using a saucer for dirt pots. The most important area indoor is along the baseboards of the walls and as high as one foot up the wall. Bleach can kill Powdery Mildew spores and keep insects away. Flies can carry smaller insects piggy backing, such as spider mites. Outdoor medical mj farmers can also bleach outside once per month for the same reason. Walkways and paths that the farmer uses around the house and the farm can be sprayed once a week with the bleach solution on ground or floors. In Colorado, a good chance exists you will be walking at another medical mj farm. There is also the chance that you could go to a medical-marijuana dispensary. A dispensary could have people present who are around all kinds of medical mj. Spraying bleach solution as a preventative can cut down chances of Powdery Mildew and spider mite problems in the great state of Colorado.

Using a 350-gallon tank for mixing nutrient solution and a hose with a valve, hand feed individual medical mj plants. Some may not have the energy for this. The ideology is that on a hand feed, the plants get individual inspection. Only a quick look takes place because two things are being done at once. I go through a second time that day and do a second inspection. The second inspection is more thorough and while sitting on a five-gallon bucket.

On the second inspection, a tool belt is worn. Not a big tool belt, one big enough to hold two sizes of trimming scissors. I prefer Hydro farm for scissors in the field and trimming. Their tools are more durable and they have a better assortment of small hand scissors. I like one pair big enough to trim whole branches off the medical mj plant and one small enough to cut leaves. Other tools in my tool belt are white plastic pylon markers with a black marker for placing a note on a specific plant (example, plant may need *CALMAG*). Another useful thing in a tool belt is bright-colored plastic ribbon. This marker ribbon is usually yellow, red, neon orange, and can be found in various other colors. It is useful if spider mites or Powdery Mildew are located on a plant. If so, mark a top portion of the plant with ribbon. It can be seen from a distance and you can come back to it, easily identified.

A quality magnifying glass is common in the tool belt. Twistie ties can be found at the grocery store for twist tying produce bags. These are used to tie various branches of the plant to bamboo supports. For example, the medical mj plants main trunk is not growing straight and needs to be straightened upright because the plant is growing crooked. It is important to train the medical mj plant to grow straight up/ standing up straight, and not leaning over. When it becomes heavy with buds, it will support the weight of the buds better when standing up straight. The twist ties may also be used to support individual branches with bamboo supports for those with extra heavy buds. Sometimes a branch may need to be supported/adjusted in the vegetative stage to allow light to a lower branch for maximum yield. Slight branch adjusting is not to be confused with bending, a technique not advised, because it can cause plant stress, possibly affecting maximum yield.

Always concentrate on an inspection for spider mites and Powdery Mildew when doing one of these weekly chores:

* A second inspection can also take place on a day when amending/conditioning soil with extra fertilizers. Add at half-strength an additional tablespoon of bat guano and chicken manure to the dirt just before Labor Day. Always try to kill two birds with one stone when visiting/ inspecting a medical mj plant. Being thorough does not hurt.

* Grooming medical mj plants will help the plant get taller in the vegetative stage. In the flower stage it will do the same thing, but also send the much more present flowering hormones up to the middle and top of the plant, where bud growth is the best. The best way to groom medical mj plants is to go to the very bottom branch or very bottom two branches and completely cut them off at the base of the trunk, especially if the leaves of these low-lying branches are sitting in the medium or dirt. These leaves give extra spots for bugs to crawl onto the plant and leaves can get yellow in dirt, allowing for a mold situation to be a potential.

* A second daily inspection can be done on a day when grooming lower and middle branches takes place. Lower branches tend to only have one to two good buds on them, so if you cut all the other sucker branches off the very lower branches, this insures a bigger, denser bud out on the very end of a lower branch. On the middle branches, keep in mind the buds on the end of the branch will get the most development also, because the plant naturally draws up nutrients through the roots and pushes them out to the very end of branches and to the top of the plant.

- A second inspection can be done on a day when you trim leaves. Leaf removal would only take place if the leaf is yellowing, unhealthy, or has a leaf miner or other unwanted bug infesting the leaf. Leaves are only removed if they do not appear to get healthy again. It is always a good idea to have your medical marijuana plants groomed of any unnecessary leaves. If for some reason you have to spray the crop, you'll use less spray that will be used on unwanted leaves and you will not be struggling to spray healthy leaves that are blocked by yellow or unnecessary vegetation. This will save you time and money if spraying of any kind is necessary.
- A medical mj farmer has many things he could do on the second inspection in order to get it done thoroughly. Outdoor or indoor medical mj farmers using pots with dirt can go through and give the pot a third to half turn so medical mj plants get bright light on all sides.
- Another inspection can involve checking for sex on all plants in the vegetative stage, even if the plant is known to be a female clone from a female mother. When growing a large medical mj crop, never assume that you have a one-hundred-percent female crop. A quick inspection is always a good idea all through the vegetative stage. If an accident occurs during flower stage and a bud gets knocked off the plant, break it open and inspect for seeds. If there is a seed, you may be able

to correct problems before getting to harvest. Breaking the bud open allows to see if any types of bugs are making a home to your medicine and letting you address the issue.

- When using dirt/ soil pots outdoors, consider aerating the medium. It will be obvious when needed, because there will be so many roots in your pot, the pot contents gets very dense. The density will not allow the water and nutrients you are feeding the medical mj plant to *flood* through the pot as fast as usual, if at all. You will physically have to aerate the medium with a hand tool, such as a galvanized steel rod, so you can remain standing. A golf club with the club cut off works as well. Be very careful not to punch holes in your pot/ container or your nutrient solution will drain out the puncture instead of flooding through the medium/ soil to the drain holes at the bottom of the pot. Do not be afraid to hurt the roots. Break up and loosen your medium/ soil so there is some air in it. This chore is less physical on your body if the pots/ containers have been freshly watered and the medium is wet. Your tool will aerate through easier. On indoor-farming set ups, aeration stones are used with a connecting air hose from an air pump. The air stones *do* get clogged from algae eventually. Having a back-up set of air stones is a good idea. Once you have decided the stones are not allowing efficient aeration, then take the dirty ones off, and slip on the clean back-up stones. Algae-clogged air stones can be cleaned by boiling in water.

- Use a flush on all indoor and outdoor crops fourteen days prior to harvest. I use a flush of water and molasses to flush nutrients in the medium and the plant so the taste of organic and nonorganic fertilizers and chemicals will not be in the MMJ end product. This can be done more often than less. On the flush prior to harvest I will flush at least two times per day, morning and night.

17

Foresight

When self employed, there is always something you can be doing work wise.

Foresight is about managing your own business. Look down the road and start on prep so it's not as much work when it actually has to be done. For example: You had it easy during vegetative stage. You have flower season approaching. Do you have your lattice ready for supporting your heavy buds? If not using lattice, do you have your bamboo supports ready and in stock? Do you have your choice of flower hardener in stock? Although rare now, at times during the medical mj boom during 2009-2011, some nutrients and even some kinds of dirt could be out of stock for weeks. Get your arsenal months before you need it. Do you have your drying, curing, trimming area ready? Do you have your patients ready? Do you have your people for bud trimming? Good bud trimmers make good money if they can trim a pound or more a day. Try to find at least one who's this skilled so you can have the other bud trimmers try to keep up with the race-horse. Do you have your compost area ready?

Looking down the road is a valuable skill.

Trimming Buds

A couple different ways exist to approach this cat. In California, it is pretty common to cut down the entire plant at harvest and hang it upside down in a cool dark room for two- three weeks. Use plenty of ventilation and a dehumidifier if the moisture is going to cause mold problems.

In Colorado it is common to flush with treated water or a water/molasses mix for two to three weeks before cutting down the girls. It is also common in Colorado to trim wet buds and then dry the buds after they are trimmed. I prefer the method of trimming dry or just a tad from fully dry. There is plus and minus to both techniques. We will start with pros and cons of trimming wet, then pros and cons of trimming dry.

TRIMMING MEDICAL-MJ BUDS WET.

This technique is common because the need for drying rooms with space for the entire plant to dry means less real estate. You can remove upper mature buds for trimming and leave lower buds growing another two weeks. The drawback to trimming wet buds is that it is messy because of the stickiness of the fresh resins, crystals, trichomes that will get on the hands of trimmers. Bud-trimming machines are available in Colorado for daily rental or purchase. The plus to the machine is that it is useful for very large crops. Only freshly cut wet buds can be used in bud-trimming machines. Most importantly, only the dense strains of buds will survive the bud-trimming machine.

Fluffy medical-mj buds will only be destroyed in a bud-trimming machine. They will be reduced to shake and the machines are not advised for the beginner or novice medical mj farmer.

Either way, whether using a bud-trimming machine or trimming buds wet by hand, the finished bud product has to be dried before it is cured. Drying the buds can be done in inexpensive bud-drying racks that hang from the ceiling like a hanging plant does. A cheaper way is to just go to the liquor store and get a bunch of cardboard flats for free. These cardboard flats hold two twelve packs of beer. They are basically cardboard trays for medical mj buds.

Place these cardboard flats in a line on the floor. Place a cheap window fan at one end of the cardboard flats and dry your buds. Every six to twelve hours stir the buds in the cardboard flats so all sides of the bud dries. *Rubber Maid* and all the other bigger-container companies have made a lot of extra money in Colorado and California. These containers are known as bud boxes in medical marijuana country. The forty-five gallon bud box is also a common size. Store your buds in these boxes once the buds are dry.

TRIMMING MEDICAL MJ BUDS DRY.

Having rooms prepared for drying is ideal. It is also handy to have a dry room with ten-foot high ceilings. One whole level of plants can be hung to dry high up by the ceiling. A whole different level can be hung to dry below that by running five to six foot lengths of string down from the ceiling. Attach the low-hanging plants to the string. Make sure to install large fans up by the ceiling and couple low at floor level. Have plenty of wall vents and two dehumidifiers if necessary. The slow dry of an entire plant is better for buds than that of a quick dry.

These are commonly known as bud box's in Colorado.
The black bud box could also be used as a plant pot/container.

Trimming dry buds in a machine is not presently possible. But hand- trimmed buds still have a high demand. Many complaints occur on the quality of the trim job done by machines. The quality of trimming can affect the return of customers. Some medical-mj farmers may frown on the technique of wetting dried buds. I only do this practice to keep dry buds from crumbling when being handled by trimmers. Ideally plants that are hanging upside down to dry are easier to trim when just a tad wet. Unfortunately, if growing a large crop, only a portion of it will be trimmed slightly wet. Most of the crop will completely dry before it gets trimmed. For plants that are beyond dry, take a forty-five gallon container with a lid (bud box).

Cut the branches off a dried plant and place into the bud box. As you go, spray lightly $H2O$ on every third of the way up the container. Put the lid on and set over night. This will wet the buds just enough to make them an easy trim for next day. By leaving buds on branches, the moisture wets branches and buds, and after trimming, these dry buds will dry over night. This wetting process keeps the dry buds from getting over handled by bud trimmers, resulting in less trim and more bud.

CURING.

A couple of ways exist to approach this cat. Some prefer to use large mason jars and put dried medical-mj buds in the mason jars. The mason jar is then opened every twenty-four to forty-eight hours to breathe. The time that the lid is left off the mason jar varies, but fifteen minutes to two hours works. The lid is then placed back on the mason jar for another twenty-four to forty-eight hours. This breathing process can take place for months if you have that kind of time, but one - two weeks works. This process intensifies the aroma of fresh medical mj buds.

The *Food Saver* vacuum seal machine works best. The packaging of medical mj buds in *Food Saver* bags is a common practice in

Colorado. A common unit size per vacuum seal bag is one pound. The pound of medical mj should be weighed over a pound by one/quarter ounce for this curing process. Leave the dried medical mj buds vacuum-sealed for twenty-four to forty-eight hours. Open the vacuum seal bag and put the contents in a bud box for fifteen-minutes to two hours to breathe. Place the buds back in the vacuum seal bag and seal. Repeat this process for up to two weeks. This vacuum seal bag is a larger container than a mason jar and will not break like a glass jar. The drawback is that you will lose about four grams of shake from handling larger amounts of medical mj buds. You will get some shake from mason jar curing also. This is where super dense buds are best. The dense bud holds up to packaging much better. Do *not* throw away trim. If you don't use it, you can sell it in Colorado. It has value.

19

Trim And The Various Bi-Products

An incredible amount of medical-mj bi-products are being made in the great state of Colorado. Let's first start with some numbers that have been speculated on edible use during the medical-mj boom, the years 2007-2011. One statistic came up with these facts: Twenty percent of the population that has absolutely no interest in smoking medical marijuana, *and* has never tried medical marijuana, is willing to try an edible.[13] This statement is accurate. The general population in the USA and in the world has no interest in smoking anything. Things have changed a lot in the last fifty years for health reasons and the reputation of corporate tobacco companies and the government. The interest in medical marijuana has increased, and for those who want to try an edible because they do not want to smoke, hallelujah.

The statistics on edible use has risen since 2007-2011. That is due to an increase in production on all the medical-marijuana and MMJ bi-products since those years of the boom. By the way, Colorado may be in another boom since legal pot was introduced to the world and the great state of Colorado as of January 1, 2014.[9]

The fact that the US population has decreased the tobacco use in the last fifty years has been because of laws prohibiting smoking in a lot of public areas. The main reason people do not smoke tobacco is because of exorbitant taxation on a pack of cigarettes. Tobacco is not socially acceptable as it was fifty years ago, mostly for health reasons. Marijuana smoke does not have the negative health effects of tobacco. Most tobacco in cigarette form has been documented to have many added addictive chemicals.

Lets get back to medical-marijuana bi-products. Let me first state that this book will really only scratch the surface when it comes to mj bi-products. Although bi-products have been around a long time, new products are in the works all the time. You would really have to specialize just in bi-products to be an expert. For example, many people just specialize in the tetrahydrocannabinol(CBD)strains of medical-mj and the bi-products from those CBD strains. There is already a lot of specialization in the medical-marijuana industry. The reason is because that baking itself is a skill/trade. Bakers making brownies and other eatable medicine specialize. Not all citizens can bake, farm, bud trim, etc. Each skilled area may dabble in another area but some individuals know what their callings are and can only do so much in a day.

The best bi-products come from what is called sugar trim. This is trim from medical-marijuana buds. For example, you are curing buds and you have some high quality shake or sugar trim left over. Another resource for sugar trim is medical mj buds from a medical mj plant that did not turn out as good as the rest of the ninety-eight percent of the crop. Somebody has to be the runt. A small plant or trying to grow a new strain of mj may not have equaled the rest of the harvest in quality and gets used as sugar trim.

There are lesser qualities of medical-mj trim. Do not throw it out. This trim is what is left on the tarp on the floor, after a trimming crew trimmed six plants for eight hours. This trim does have sugar trim in it, but also has some leaf material. The leaves can be picked out later. This trim is ideal for products such as Pot Butter. We will refer to the two different kinds of trim as: 1) sugar-trim and 2) trim.

HASH OIL.

Many ways exist to make hash oil. Only one way will be taught in this book. I see the hash-oil-making process as dangerous in most cases.

Butane extraction is probably the most popular in Colorado. Butane extraction will not be explained in this book.

I chose another technique of hash-oil making, because the products needed are inexpensive and easy to obtain in most cases, and can be done at home. Hash oil is usually smoked. In Colorado, it is also used to make some edibles such as chocolates and is valuable as it can strengthen other edible products, which will be explained in Tincture.

First start by purchasing a gallon of Everclear grain alcohol. For all you Tennessee boys, you can use moonshine. They both work. (If you have the budget, Hexanol is the best food-grade alcohol product you can purchase for this project.)

Get as big a mason jar as you can find. Put as much sugar trim in the mason jar as possible. If you have buds, then grind them up to the consistency of sugar trim (the consistency of coffee grinds). A hand held- bud grinder works or you can use a clean coffee-bean grinder. Once you have the mason jar full with as much sugar trim as possible, add your Everclear. Fill the mason jar slowly to about eighty-five to ninety-percent full. Put the lid on snug. Put the mason jar and its contents on its side in the freezer. Every twelve hours look at the mason jar in the freezer. When looking at the mason jar for the first day or two, do not touch it. You should see after looking closely at the mason jar on its side in the freezer, a thin layer of oil on top of the alcohol. Once you see the layer of oil floating on top of the alcohol, you can alternate six hours at room temperature, then six hours back in the freezer. It is okay to agitate the contents for a minute when going back to the freezer at this point. This process works better the longer you do it but two weeks is satisfactory. After two weeks all the oil from the veg matter will be floating on top of the entire contents of the mason jar.

What is nice about this process is that it does not need to be done all in one day's work.

The next step is to take a coffee filter and the funnel it fits in, and place it over a container with a mouth to catch most of the strained contents. I like to place a large bowl under this container to catch anything that slips out. Have a clean glass container with a lid ready to catch your alcohol/ oil mix. Make sure to wear latex or rubber gloves before working. This will prevent your hands from staining dark green. Squeeze the sugar trim, alcohol/ hash oil mix as hard as you can to get all the alcohol and hash oil out of the sugar trim. Get another coffee filter ready because only a few tablespoons at one time will go through one coffee filter before the coffee filter is unusable and the new one will be necessary to process the entire mason jar. Be careful not to squeeze so hard to bust the coffee filter or you will have to filter the sugar trim all over again. Which is not a bad idea, anyway. You can also try double up on the coffee filter. (Industrial fry-oil filters for filtering restaurant deep fryer oil work better than coffee filters.)

Be sure to have all your vegetable matter filtered out before moving to this step. The next step is the dangerous part, because you are cooking (double boiling) grain alcohol on the kitchen stove. But before you start that, take a small portion of your grain- alcohol/ hash-oil mix (two shots or more) and put this in some vodka to make marijuana vodka. It's technically not vodka because it has grain alcohol in it. That's why we call it marijuana vodka. About two shots to a pint of vodka is all you need. The last step is where you cook off the alcohol to have your final hash-oil product. Set up on your kitchen stove or a camp stove outside. If using the kitchen have your exhaust fan on with windows open and fire extinguisher nearby, just in case. The idea on this process is to have plenty of ventilation so the alcohol fumes do not catch fire. Put a large frying pan or saucepan on the stove with water in it. Put a Pyrex glass container big enough to hold all of your grain-alcohol/ hash-oil mix, in center of the saucepan. Set stove at a temperature to double boil.

Technically, you could skip the whole cooking process and let the alcohol evaporate off of the hash oil. This process would take weeks, most likely. I have not tried the evaporation method, but if you used a fan to speed the process, it would probably work.

Only double boil your grain-alcohol/ hash-oil mix to the consistency of motor oil. (This process is similar to a sauce chef doing a reduction after a deglaze with a wine. You are cooking off the alcohol. If you are not a former sauce chef and in doubt, it's better to leave some alcohol in than over cooking. Much like in comparison to a sauté` dish.)

Now that you have your hash oil in a Pyrex bowl, you can leave it there or scrape the hash-oil into a small container with a lid. Use one scraping tool only, so you are not losing hash-oil on various hand tools. Leave the lid off the hash-oil container for a couple days. This lets any residual grain alcohol in the hash-oil evaporate. You will smell grain alcohol if there is residual. At least it is an edible grain alcohol instead of other alcohols. Hexanol is very expensive, but is mainstream in Colorado and allows for nice clear hash-oil.

Back to your Pyrex glass bowl. Let the residual hash-oil dry on the Pyrex and scrape it off later. The process to let it dry could take a long time, but this dried hash-oil is a trendy product in Colorado called Shatter. It is smoked like hash with buds or tossed in coffee. You can take your finished hash-oil and smoke it, or you can ingest it by making a batch of chocolate kisses. What is truly incredible about medical-mj edibles is that they all have a different buzz/medicinal characteristic.

TINCTURE   Medical-marijuana tincture is one of my favorite medicines. The high/ buzz wears off the cleanest, like you never dosed. The medical-mj tincture product is made many different ways. This is a common recipe.

Start with a product found in health stores called vegetable glycerin. This can be found most economically priced on the

Internet. The best vegetable glycerin found for your buck is *Essential* brand, and it is also kosher. One of the characteristics of vegetable glycerin is that it tastes very similar to honey.

Next, grab your crockpot and fill it halfway or less with vegetable glycerin depending on how much sugar trim you have. Put as much sugar trim as you can in to the crockpot with the vegetable glycerin. You will only need the low setting for the entire six to twelve hours you cook it. Stir it frequently. Do not burn it and do not worry about making it too strong. You can always make it stronger or weaker in medicine content.

After you have cooked it on low for six to twelve hours, let the crock-pot cool to room temperature. Prepare a large bowl big enough to hold a spaghetti strainer. Line the spaghetti strainer with cheese-cloth and pour a portion of your crockpot into the cheese clothe using a ladle. Squeeze and strain the vegetable glycerin through the cheesecloth. Do not let any sugar-trim/ vegetable matter get passed the cheesecloth. We are making medical-marijuana medicine. Take pride in your finished product.

Before you bottle this product, sample the tincture to see if it is incredibly potent or mild. Cover the bowl of finished tincture product with plastic wrap while you're medicating.

I like to put the finished tincture medicine in half ounce or one ounce bottles. But before you bottle it, decide how strong you want your medicine to be. Do you want one drop of the tincture to be the dose? Or do you want four to six drops to be the dose? With a six-drop dose, you will taste the honey sweetness of the tincture more than with a one-drop dose.

I recommend two batches. Make one sweet for Xmas gifts and one very potent for the shelf, for everyday use. The less-potent batch can be cut with more plain vegetable glycerin. The stronger batch needs to be put back in to a clean crockpot on low for one hour or two with six to twelve drops of hash oil. This is where a journal is useful. If you make it too strong, people usually do not complain and it can always be cut with more fresh vegetable glycerin. The strong batch will be effective with one drop under the tongue or two drops in coffee. Once you have your half ounce bottles, prepare an assembly line. I like to use a sun tea container with a faucet/ tap. These can be found at department stores. Pour your mild batch in to the sun tea container and fill your bottles with tincture then strong batch. I have found this to be the least messy, and the least wasteful.

DRY ICE KEIF

Keif is also known as pollen and keif hash. In this book the instructions will be given for dry ice keif because I think it's the least labor intensive of the hash-making processes.

Prepare your work area where dust is not going to be a problem (example, garage or basement). Start with a worktable. This can be as simple as a set of sawhorses with a half or full sheet of plywood across it. A coffee table also works. Put a clean piece of poly plastic on your worktable. You can use various silkscreen set ups, but the same silkscreen bags that fit in a five-gallon bucket, used for making bubble hash work well. These bags are known as bubble bags in the medical mj industry. Have your sugar trim and dry ice ready and near by your worktable. When using a bubble bag select the one with the biggest holes, not the finest screen. If you do not have enough sugar trim for a five-gallon bucket, then use a coffee can.

Fill the five-gallon bucket with a third full of sugar trim. Break up approximately three to five pounds of dry ice into smaller pieces the size of ice cubes or bigger. Put the dry ice in the five-gallon bucket with the trim. Pull your bubble bag over the five-gallon bucket so it goes over the outside, and the silk screen at the bottom of the bag is tight around the opening. Use a violent shaking motion with the bucket upside down and the opening being screened onto your clean plastic sheet on your worktable. Shake the bucket violently as in the motion of trying to empty the contents of the bucket on to the worktable.

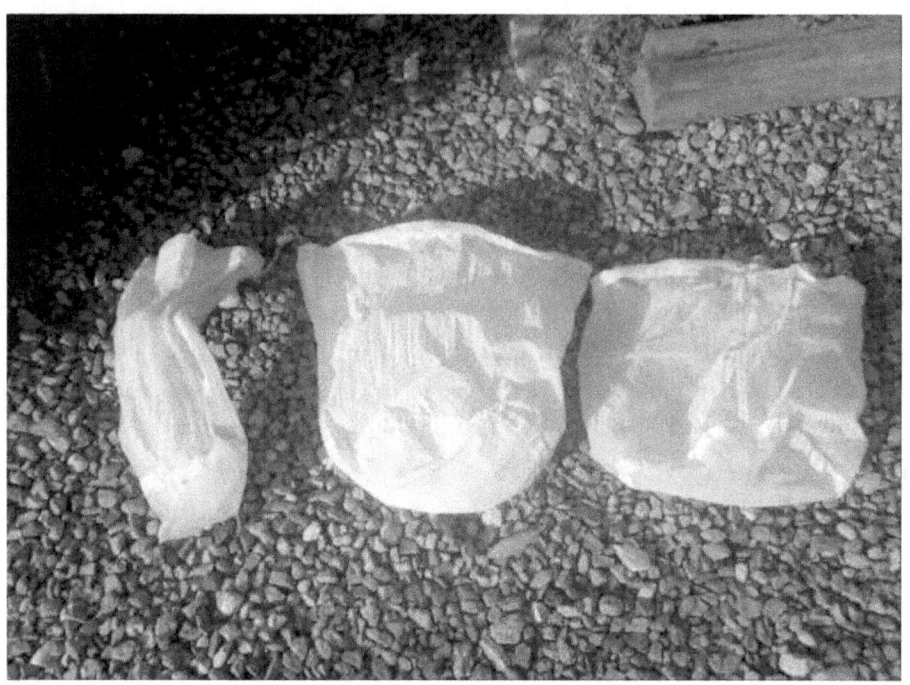

Silk-screen BUBBLE BAGS. You may need to take a trip to
Colorado to see how the bubble bags are used and medicate while you're at it.

You may want to use work gloves because the dry ice can make the bucket cold. You can change out the bucket with fresh sugar trim. Re use any dry ice. Save the used sugar trim. It can be run through the silkscreen a second time or used in pot butter. Scrape up your kief from your worktable with a credit card. For a professional look put it through a hash press. You will most likely have to let your keif/pollen dry out for a couple days. The dry ice can be so cold that it will add some moisture. If you are a beginner and your bi-products turn out less than desirable, never throw them out. Almost every medical mj bi-product can be put in brownies and cookies or any food or drink to add medicinal qualities. Undesirable keif can be made into the form of THC *pills.* Empty edible gel capsules can be purchased from health food stores or on the Internet. Put your keif in the gel capsules. Start with a one-pill dose. If it's not strong enough, then increase the dose accordingly.

POT BUTTER AND OLIVE OIL

Medical-marijuana olive oil is one of my all-time favorites. Have a wild dinner party? You can put olive oil in pasta, salad, stir-fry, sautéed mushrooms and onions on a NY strip steak, etc. If you have a wild dinner party, where every dish has medical-mj olive oil or pot butter in it, please have space for guests to stay overnight instead of driving.

Medical mj olive oil is made the same way pot butter is made. The beauty of medical-mj olive oil is that it needs no refrigeration or freezer for storage. Vegetable oil is much cheaper, but does not hold up to heat as well as olive oil. Vegetable oil will brown in color in the process of cooking it with medical-mj trim. Brown medical-mj oil is perfectly acceptable for cooking in baked goods such as brownies, cookies, granola bars, etc. because the brown medical-mj oil will never be seen in these edible products. The making of medical-mj olive oil is more so for gifts and does hold up to heat and keeps its clear olive-oil color. The cost difference of vegetable oil and olive oil is substantial for this process.

Pot Butter, olive oil, and vegetable oil are all made the same way. The general rule is: If you use a gallon of vegetable oil, you will lose one/half gallon in the process of making it, leaving you with a final-product of one/half gallon, depending on how much trim you have. Let's start with a gallon of vegetable oil. The cheapest brand can be purchased for less than nine dollars per gallon. Get your crockpot and fill it half way with vegetable oil. Add trim close to the top of the crockpot. The trim will saturate with oil and you have to add oil and trim accordingly to have a mixture consistency that you can stir. You never have to use a setting of more than low heat on all medical-mj bi-products. After six to twelve hours, let your medicine cool. The dreaded cheesecloth is needed. Use nice bottles for medical mj olive-oil gifts. The gallon jug that the vegetable oil was purchased in can be reused for vegetable oil. Same guidelines apply to oil and butter making, as in the tincture guidelines: If the oil is too strong in potency it can be watered down and weakened in strength with fresh butter or oil. If it needs more potency then a few drops of hash oil can be added. Every batch will vary in MMJ strength due to the potency of the trim and the maker of the oil or butter. The maker/farmer of the bi-products may have an idea of how strong the oil or butter will be based on the quality of the trim or buds being used. The general rule is one teaspoon of oil or butter per dose. A baker of baked medicine such as brownies or cookies should have the edible portions of medicine in bite-sized doses (one inch x one inch). This way a patient can eat two brownies if he has a higher tolerance to THC. Some caregivers make their bi-products very strong and some like to eat lots of food and make their edibles weaker in THC content. The best way is to take masking tape and a black marker and mark your containers medium or strong. Smaller containers of one/half ounce bottles can be stored in smaller boxes with markings on the box to indicate the strength of that particular medicine.

Edible forms of MMJ are notorious for being excellent sleeping aids. The three drawbacks to edibles are: 1) they can take a half hour to one hour to take effect unlike smoking, where the effects are almost instant. 2) Some people that do not use edibles on a regular basis can experience a *hangover* the following morning or day from a strong MMJ edible. 3) One out of ten people will not be able to experience the medical relief of a digested edible, do to their body chemistry that does not allow their intestines to absorb the THC into their bloodstream.

If a first time user of an edible eats a brownie that is too strong to his liking he can eat a sandwich or meal to try to dilute the THC content in his bloodstream, similar to someone who has had too much alcohol too drink.

I think that all forms of MMJ medication have different highs. I like edibles for insomnia. A very strong edible could be used if someone has been in an accident and should not be moving around due to severe physical injuries. All marijuana and marijuana products should not be left out where small children can get these medicines in their mouths. Medical marijuana brownies, cookies, etc., can be mistaken for regular snacks or goodies by children and adults. Colorado has many cases documented in the media from small children getting into MMJ medicine by accident and older children playing pranks on other children by giving them a strong edible, resulting in illness. Pranks are an act of poisoning. Anyone thinking of trying a prank such as this may want to think twice.

It's unfortunate that marijuana has made it this far to get smeared in the media due to someone's negligence or prank. It is important to see that many other drugs can cause these very same problems in the public.

There currently are no Colorado regulations for caregivers to label the strength of their MMJ bi-products. However the state of Colorado has come up with regulations for dispensaries and the recreational pot stores. The process first starts through a second-party testing lab.

Although all medical marijuana bi-products are labor intensive, hopefully people around you will appreciate these recipes. All medicines have value and can be sold or traded for other items. For example, your best bud trimmer is appreciated for setting the pace for you and your other bud trimmers, so you give tincture medicine as a weekly bonus. By the way, tincture is excellent in tea and coffee. The author can be consulted on the very many topics in this book.

20

Security

Security cameras and a DVR can be set up at an inexpensive cost. The Chinese brands are usually a counterfeit of a very good brand such as Sony. Mom and Pop security-camera companies can usually give you this inside information on which is the best off-name product. Purchase signs. Smile, you are on Camera or Surveillance Cameras. If people, including cops, see camera signs, they will have a completely different behavior from normal. Security cameras are the way of the future for all.

It would be rare for law enforcement to show up at your property in the great state of Colorado for growing medical marijuana. You would have to be disturbing the peace, or have a lot of odor, or a neighbor who has called in anonymously complaining of odor. There is no crime for odor. It is not uncommon for police to come over if someone does call in anonymously for odor. They will come over to check that your medical-mj paperwork is up to date. In the case of medical mj or recreational pot they may want to have a look on your property to do a plant count to see that you are not over the amount that you are allowed. You do *not* have to let them on the property for *any* reason. The bottom line is that they need to have a warrant to come to your property. If they have a warrant, then they presented reasonable cause to a judge, who issued the warrant. A false police report is not allowed by neighbors or anyone else. The main purpose of security cameras is to send a sign to law enforcement that they will have to follow the law. Most times, if law enforcement shows up to check your paperwork, and they see that you have security cameras, they will not even step on to the property but rather wait in the street for you.

Part of the reason it's *legal* to grow medical marijuana in Colorado is because police have not followed procedure in the past, and have had lawsuits against them and lost. Most cases are of police confiscating medical-mj plants, which in a courtroom or anywhere else are considered medicine. Thereby restitution is awarded to the defendant/ the caregiver. If the police do not follow procedure, plenty of good medical-marijuana attorneys practice in Colorado.

If, for example, the authorities come to your front door and you answer, they will most likely want to enter or do a plant count. They are not allowed in or on the property without a warrant or from your permission. Do not be afraid to answer that you are in the middle of something with your guests, and would be happy to set an *appointment* with them. If police get aggressive, then you can use the words: You need a warrant to be on the property. Also, it is not against the law to *not* answer the door. Not answering the door can be first option on your list. Never be stand off-ish with law enforcement. Law enforcement tend to force themselves on young people more than adults. This is called intimidation.

If you do not have the budget for security cameras, then go to a Mom and Pop security store and ask if they have some that are being thrown out that no longer work. If you install them on the property, be certain to run a cable out the wall to the camera. Make it look like a real set-up and do maintenance if a beehive is in a camera. Some people pay attention to details. Decoys can make people think differently.

Make copies of your current medical marijuana paperwork in triplicate. This would be the paper work with your doctor's signature, medical license number, and the extended plant count. Also, a copy of the actual Red Card and a copy of your driver's license or ID. Place one set of copies in a ziploc plastic bag, then another ziploc plastic bag, so this copy is double bagged. Place your water-resistant copy of your medical marijuana paperwork somewhere outside. For example, in the garage, or an automobile, or under something large where it will not get moist. This duplicate copy you can present to law enforcement if they stop by while you are outside. Do not give them a reason to look around while you are shuffling around for paperwork. Keeping an eye on what is going on is hard if you are shuffling around for paperwork.

Place one copy in your home, and another in the medical-marijuana farm area. It also helps to place a copy in your vehicle or vehicles. Social security numbers are on the papers that are mailed to the Colorado Medical Marijuana Registry. Make sure to cross off all the social security numbers except the last four digits, just in case these documents get in the wrong hands.

Handling officers of the law should not be a problem unless you are doing something illegal. It is a violation of the law in Colorado to have any other drugs on the property unless, they have been prescribed by a doctor. Firearms and marijuana are Federal offenses.[14] If you need the security, use pepper spray.

Firearms and marijuana equals a bad choice. Also, dog lovers, Pit Bulls are illegal in the city limits of Denver.

Keep cash in a safe. Always try to keep less than $10,000.00 in your safe. A gang box, otherwise known as a job-site toolbox is useful for the storage of medical marijuana in your home. Put medical marijuana in vacuum-sealed food bags before placing it in the gang box. Large gun safes are heavy and expensive.

Pepper spray is a better choice than a firearm.

This is an Amsec brand safe. It will keep your
girlfriend from doing something you might want to dump her for.

Security is primarily to make law enforcement act like people instead of Nazis. It also makes your friends think twice if you have them over. Call me paranoid, but I like to meet friends for a burger so they are not over. General rule– don't stay away from home very long. Having a safe just buys you time.

21

The Black Market

As most people know, marijuana was around well before medical marijuana or Colorado recreational pot. It has been known among marijuana farmers for decades that marijuana has more value than most other crops. It has been and will remain of value. The fact that marijuana has value is no secret any more. A pound of marijuana can be currently valued at approximately $2,600.00. This information is from the website, California Medical Marijuana - NORML.org. Then go to the right column under California Laws and Information, then, click Crop Data. There you will see California's top-ten cash crops. This data is outdated, but still very much in the ballpark. Marijuana's real value from year to year is determined by supply and demand. Since Colorado is ahead of other states by over a decade, it will probably lead the industry. Every state in the USA may not choose to adopt medical marijuana, but every state in the USA does not allow same-sex marriages. Choose to live in the state you want to live in.

The first reason I decided to get into the business of medical marijuana was because of the research on marijuana case law. A lot of people were transporting marijuana before the medical marijuana boom. In many cases, where a citizen with a good attorney had no prior criminal records, specifically felony records, received sentences of probation for driving with pounds of marijuana from California to Utah or Colorado to Illinois, etc. These cases all involved less than one hundred pounds of marijuana. The individuals in these cases also received no jail sentences.

I do not suggest trying to transport marijuana across state lines. Colorado police have all beefed up their forces with as many K-9 units as they can get their hands on as well as all the surrounding states bordering Colorado. Big revenue.

The second reason I decided to get into the medical marijuana business is because of cases of Colorado caregivers getting restitution for medical-marijuana plants, from incidents where police cut down crops in the early years of the MMJ boom. Restitution was awarded to caregivers based on the fact that law enforcement destroyed the medicine of patients. Some restitution awards were in amounts of $200,000.00 and $280,00.00.

When medical-marijuana dispensaries opened, the city police would serve hand-delivered letters from the mayor to cease business. It was nerve racking for some dispensary owners during the medical-marijuana boom of 2004 to 2008. The state of Colorado had very few regulations in place during those years. As a dispensary owner, you were not certain if you were going to get raided by authorities. But most owners took a chance due to the large number of medical-marijuana dispensaries that were opening. The cities have definitely done their research to see that no owners have criminal backgrounds and that they are not part of organized crime. Part of the decision for law-abiding citizens, with no criminal records, to get into the dispensary business was due to several cases where individual caregivers had been awarded restitution for their patients' medicine, which had been raided and destroyed by authorities. This opened the legal basis for a business model. The fact that medical marijuana holds strength in a courtroom as medicine has left a lot of room for additional marijuana case law and how governments and police act on any given situation.

22

Real Estate Guidelines

You can't just think about it, you have to make a plan. First you need to get on the state of Colorado map. For outdoor farming, the front-range is a better choice. The cool climate and very short summer at altitude will not give you a yield you can be satisfied with. For the indoor grower, altitude has been known to aid in a higher production of trichomes/ crystals on buds. For the indoor grower, the outdoor crop is additional annual income.

Homes that are valued at $200,000 to $300,000 in the Denver area and suburbs are in a sellers' market. If it's an MMJ property, then it's a whole different sellers' market. I only know one realtor who markets himself as a marijuana realtor and he does primarily commercial warehouses for grow facilities for dispensaries. The MMJ network is like a cult and most residential properties are found word of mouth.

The first rule is to plan your grow so that you're the only one who knows about it. Bud trimmers should be restricted to a trimming area and normally do not get to see an entire grow inside and out. They are just trimmers not farmers. Most businessmen do not invite anyone to look at their business inside and out, no matter what kind of business.

The second rule is to know the town, city, or county ordinances for plant counts and if there are restrictions on amounts that can be grown. If you plan on growing outside, research if there is a current policy in effect for outdoor growing. Never have outdoor plants visible from the street, and save yourself headaches by keeping out-door plants out of view of neighbors from any property line. If neighbors can see your outdoor plants, make sure they are growing marijuana also. In general, in today's world *neighbor* is a bad word. Do not associate with neighbors if possible.

If purchasing or renting a residential property, consult a journeyman electrician on your growing plan and the amount of electricity that he suggests you will need to make your plan operate successfully. Know your electrical costs before you buy the house.

Water is usually not a problem but do a little research. You need water to farm. If on a well make sure it's not close to dry.

Basements are ideal areas for the indoor grower. Concrete floors make for easy cleanup. Basements with ten-foot high ceilings are hard to come by, but they do exist.

If renting a property, find a landlord who is marijuana friendly. MMJ has been around long enough that landlords who are biased have already written it in the lease that marijuana is not allowed to be grown on the property. Some landlords want a farming tenant. They look at it as a tenant who will most likely pay the rent. Try to get your monthly rent payment secured by getting a two or three-year lease agreement with the option to extend the lease. The biggest problem with renting is the landlord can get greedy and expect a higher monthly rent payment when your lease expires.

As of October tenth, 2014 the most-friendly areas in Colorado for the work-from-home caregiver are suburbs of Denver–Lakewood, Arvada, and Aurora.

The counties of Summit, Eagle, and Jefferson are the most friendly. The following counties are in second place to the above counties- Pueblo, El Paso, Larimer, San Miguel, Weld, and Grand.

Residential and commercial real estate that is used to grow marijuana has to be 1000 feet away from schools. Churches can be schools if they have children's classes. Do your research.

The author can be contacted for additional information or a referral.

23

In Summary

This book is the first of a series. In the twenty-four years I have been living in Colorado, my eyes have been a camera, taking pictures of the most beautiful state. Watching the evolution of marijuana in Colorado has been another picture of many to come.

Medical marijuana real estate is only one way to make money in Colorado. I only know one realtor who markets himself as specifically a marijuana realtor. A very small portion of realtors do real estate transactions related to the marijuana network. Realtors in most cases are not a resource for information on a marijuana property. Marijuana is a network of its own, much like a cult. People in the network have information on properties and it's not necessary to put this information on-line. It's currently a sellers' market and the property can usually transact in less than a week. I know a guy in Florida who paid cash for a $250,000.00 home in Colorado, just so his kids could have a job growing marijuana.

Jobs now exist in the medical-marijuana industry. Much like technology, medical marijuana provides more jobs than other field of work in this USA economy.

Some of the jobs listed and the top and bottom rate of pay one can expect to earn based on the employees I have had. A bonus of an MMJ bi-product (example, cookie, brownie, etc.) is given to my top employee of the day, sometimes to the top two employees.

1) Farmer's assistant would have to have at least seven years growing experience. A complete one-hour interview takes place to see if the potential assistant's farming recipe is remotely similar to mine. Starting pay for a farming assistant would be fourteen dollars per hour with the understanding that the first two months of employment would be a trial period with pay. If the working relationship is mutual after two months, the pay moves up to sixteen dollars per hour. The potential to make twenty dollars per hour would be a maximum income for this job with only a dollar raise per hour per year and a maximum of forty hours per week.

2) My bud trimmers start at thirteen dollars per hour. They are on a two-day tryout on their first two shifts with pay. My trimmers are required to trim a minimum of one half pound of MMJ in the course of an entire work shift. This is dry MMJ buds. An inspection of the final trimmed buds takes place at lunch and at the end of the shift. If they do not meet the half-pound quota they are cut from the trim team. One of my trimmers can trim one pound per day. He gets paid fifteen dollars per hour and gets up to one-eighth of bud medicine per shift. Most of my trimmers, including myself, can trim three quarters of a pound. They are paid fourteen per hour and if they hit a pound for the day, they get fifteen per hour with the eighth ounce.

3) Clerks (bud tenders) earn twelve dollars per hour.

4) I have paid bakers up to fifteen per hour if they can get as much done in a kitchen as I can.

If you are the entrepreneur type, this is an incomplete list of individuals related to the MMJ network. 1) medical doctor 2) attorneys 3) home remodelers 4) electricians 5) good bakers/cooks make good bi-product producers 6) etc.

Individuals still have opinions on marijuana, and as well they should. Most people who are biased will not have anything to do with individuals involved with marijuana. If the mentioned professionals and others are biased then it allows for others that are not to have more business. Much like other business, the amount of extra business is speculation based on all the factors involved (example, marketing, reputation, etc.).

Other business opportunities that are related to the marijuana network are: 1) growing-supply stores, 2) bud-trimming machine sales and rentals, 3) head shops for pipes and vaporizers, 4) dispensary tours, 5) restaurant owners have been known to open new restaurants near a dispensary due to the reputation that marijuana gives you the munchies, 6) private-testing labs for the testing of THC content in mj buds and marijuana bi-products, 7) electricians have seen significant amount of extra work for bringing electrical infrastructure up to code, both residential and commercial for indoor growing, 8) MMJ seed companies. And the list goes on.

Once a dollar goes through a marijuana transaction, it creates a domino effect/ of transactions. Examples are: 1) the dispensary owner pays his bud trimmer for the week and the employee buys gasoline and groceries. The grocery store pays its electric bill, etc. 2) The caregiver sells MMJ to a patient and takes the payment to pay his bud trimmers. The bud trimmers buy cheeseburgers at a local eatery. 3) A couple growing marijuana illegally in Florida, move to Colorado to grow legally. They pay the rent and the landlord pays the water bill and buys lunch at the restaurant, etc. Every marijuana transaction eventually creates another transaction. Additional transactions create the need for more jobs. The amount that marijuana stimulates the Colorado economy would only be speculation. The citizens who live in Colorado can actually get a better pulse on that number and I would estimate it at fifteen to twenty percent and growing.

Medical marijuana is a lucrative choice. If you do not have the stomach for the stigma of marijuana then you might consider the many who move to Colorado every year to get on a waiting list to get their medicine. The supply does not meet the demand when it comes to providing medicine for the seizure patient.

Some medical-marijuana farmers grow medical marijuana that has very little to no high. These farmers grow strains/ types that are higher in Tetrahydrocannabinol(CBD) or Cannabidol content. These types have been proven to help seizure patients and epilepsy, where other seizure medicines have had very little to no results. If you do not have a stomach for selling marijuana because it gets people high, then you can grow the types that give no high at all and relieve seizures. Charlotte's Web is one of the CBD strains of medical marijuana.

The amount of people using marijuana in Colorado is twenty percent or much more. Medical marijuana transactions do not have to take place at a dispensary. The number of recreational pot users not going to dispensaries but rather growing their own would be hard to determine. The growing at home is much cheaper than buying and there is still the thrill and satisfaction of growing at home. After all, that's where it all started. Recreational pot and MMJ transactions are hard to determine other than the numbers of transactions reported on a daily, weekly, monthly, quarterly basis at a dispensary or recreational pot store.

The amount of money that can be made would be dependent on the amount of capital one has to start a business. Even a smart business-like hobbyist can start as part-time work. The important thing to know is that you are farming and to have the green thumb mind-set. If you want to make marijuana growing your full-time work, then you have to have the business mind-set also.

Over one million voted for the legalization of marijuana. Approximately 100,000 people are on the medical-marijuana registry for medical-marijuana cards, plus or minus on a daily basis. A local Denver Newspaper reported over five million in recreational pot sales in Denver, in the first five days recreational pot was introduced for January 1rst through January 5th, 2014. As of the end of July 2014, the state of Colorado reports 18.6 million in recreational-pot-sales taxes, as well as 5.4 million in excise taxes.

The big picture is: What kind of people are the 1,383,139 voting yes for legalizing marijuana in Colorado? Do they all have dread locks? Were these eighteen-year-old voters or forty-five-year-old voters? Are they all freaks? How many are just former mj users? How many are mothers? How many are family people? How many are just businessmen? How many do not like alcohol? How many think it's good for Colorado's economy? How many think it was a good thing for revenue? Etc.

If you have further questions, then direct your comments to coloradommjrealestate@gmail.com

This book is part of a series. I will be writing more books as the Colorado regulations change year by year. This book, Colorado Marijuana Real Estate was written in the year 2013 and 2014. Sometime prior to or in the year 2015, some of the regulations for recreational pot stores are scheduled to change due to the fact the state of Colorado has to give business people who qualify the options of buying Recreational Pot retail licenses. New recreational pot stores will have the option to be stand- alone stores or wholesale growers, as long as the state legislature does not change its plan in 2014.

Although things are scheduled to change for the corporate side of marijuana, things are not scheduled to change for the work-from-home caregiver. The only thing that is scheduled to change for the caregiver is the patient number from five to ten. This has not been determined as of October 13, 2014.

If you have the passion to be involved with the marijuana network, then make a plan. Marijuana in Colorado is going to be around a long time.

References

1) Denver WestWord Blogs, Marijuana: The million dollar pot questions Denver City Council hasn't answered. By Michael Roberts. August 27,2013.
www.blogs.westword.com/latestword/2013/08/marijuana-denver-million-dollar-questions.php

2) Amendment 64: (3).b
   Amendment 64: (3).a
   Amendment 64: (3).a, 64: (3).b, and 64: (3).c
   Amendment 64: (1). b-111 and 64: (6).b
   Amendment 64: (7)
   Amendment 64: (2).d
   Amendment 64: (1).c and 64: (5).j
   Amendment 64: (4)

3) HB 13-1325 Colorado Inferences for marijuana and driving offences.

3B) Marijuana Retailers & Home Growers/ Denver Marijuana Info, January 3, 2015, http://www.colorado.gov/pacific/marijuanainfodenver/marijuana-retailers-home-growers

4) Colorado Amendment 20

5) Medical Marijuana Colorado Department of Public Health and Environment http://www.colorado.gov/pacific/cdphe/medicalmarijuana

6) The Denver Post Denver and the West, Colorado marijuana guide: 64 answers to commonly asked questions. By John Ingold Posted: 12-31-2013 www.denverpost.com/marijuana/ci_24823785/colorado-marijuana-guide-64-answers-commonly-asked-questions

7) Denver WestWord News, Alien nation: Colorado's election is out of this world. By Patricia Calhoun, October 27, 2010. www.westword.com/2010-10-28/news/alien-nation-colorado-s-election-is-out-of-this-world

8) The Denver Post, In Colorado you still can't smoke marijuana in public. By The Denver Post Editorial Board. Posted 9-30-2013 www.denverpost.com/editorials/ci/_24208910/colorado-you-still-can't-smoke-marijuana-public

9) Colorado Governor admits economy is booming. By Jeralyn Merrit Colorado criminal defense attorney dated: July 2, 2014. www.colopot.com/?cat=6

10A) Culture Magazine/ Medical Cannabis Lifestyle and News Magazine. What to Avoid When Law Enforcement Comes A-Knocking', By Ann Toney Nov. 1, 2012

10) Denver WestWord Blogs, Voters overturn dispensary ban. By William Breathes, November 8, 2012. www.blogs.westword.com/latestword/2012/11/marijuana-fort-collins-dispensary-ban-overturn.php

11) The Denver Post, Denver sets plant limits in city limits. By Jeremy P. Meyer. December 9, 2013. www.denverpost.com/news/ci 24689956/denver-limits-pot-homegrows-12-plants

12) Maximum Yield Growing Magazine

13) Survey taken by dispensary owner in Denver, Colorado. Carl Heaton from October 2008- November 2009. Survey taken on non-smoking medical patients purchasing edibles for the first time.

14) Firearms and marijuana illegal. Colorado Bureau of Investigation James Spoden.